Much Ado About Nothing

TEXT EDITOR
JEFFREY KAHAN

ADVISORY EDITORS
DAVID BEVINGTON AND PETER HOLLAND

SERIES EDITORS
MARIE MACAISA AND DOMINIQUE RACCAH

William Shakspeare

sourcebooks
mediaFusion

An Imprint of Sourcebooks Inc.®
Naperville, Illinois

Audio and photo credits are at the end of the book.

Published by Sourcebooks MediaFusion, an imprint of Sourcebooks, Inc.
P.O. Box 4410, Naperville, Illinois 60567-4410
(630) 961-3900
Fax: (630) 961-2168
www.sourcebooks.com
www.sourcebooksshakespeare.com
For more information on The Sourcebooks Shakespeare, email us at
shakespeare@sourcebooks.com.

Printed and bound in the United States of America.
LB 10 9 8 7 6 5 4 3 2 1

To students, teachers, and lovers of Shakespeare

Contents

ABOUT SOURCEBOOKS MEDIAFUSION

Launched with the 1998 *New York Times* bestseller
We Interrupt This Broadcast and formally founded in 2000,
Sourcebooks MediaFusion is the nation's leading publisher
of mixed-media books. This revolutionary imprint is dedicated
to creating original content—be it audio, video, CD-ROM,
or Web—that is fully integrated with the books we create.
The result, we hope, is a new, richer, eye-opening,
thrilling experience with books for our readers.
Our experiential books have become both bestsellers
and classics in their subjects, including poetry (*Poetry Speaks*),
children's books (*Poetry Speaks to Children*),
history (*We Shall Overcome*), sports (*And The Crowd Goes Wild*),
the plays of William Shakespeare, and more.
See what's new from us at www.sourcebooks.com.

About the Text

There are two versions of *Much Ado About Nothing*, a quarto printed in 1600 and the folio text of 1623. The folio text of 1623 is, except in minor respects, very similar to the early quarto of 1600. This text is based upon the folio version, which seems in many instances more "stage ready" than the quarto. The punctuation and the spelling of this text have been silently modernized. Significant variations as well as editorial conjectures are recorded in the notes. Editorial additions are also found within square brackets.

The punctuation and the spelling of this text have been silently modernized along the principles espoused in Stanley Wells' *Modernizing Shakespeare's Spelling* (Oxford: Clarendon Press, 1979) and his *Re-Editing Shakespeare for the Modern Reader: Based on Lectures Given at the Folger Shakespeare Library, Washington, D.C.* (Oxford and New York: Clarendon Press; Oxford University Press, 1984). The spellings of some archaic words, such as "rechate", have been retained in their original spelling. Such conservation make little or no imposition upon on our eye or ear—an archaic word is archaic, whether the spelling is modernized or not—and have the added virtue of reminding us that some words from Shakespeare's day simply have not traveled as well as others. In regard to my notes: unless referring to the current play, all Shakespeare quotations are derived from *The Riverside Shakespeare*, ed. G. Blakemore Evans. 2nd ed. (Boston and New York: Houghton Mifflin Company, 1997).

Regarding "Anthonio": most modern editions prefer "Antonio", but there is very little bibliographical justification for this modernization. The folio speech prefixes refer to "Anth." though one speech prefix at line 2188 has "Ant." The quarto refers to "Brother." There are only two references to Anthonio's name spoken aloud in the play. At line 519 in the folio (2.1.86 in this edition):

Vrsula. I know you well enough, you are Signior An-thonio.

At 2178 in the Folio (5.1.90 in our text), he is called "Brother Anthony." In both instances, the quarto agrees with folio. So, overwhelmingly, our character's name is "Anthony" or "Anthonio." All this being said, modern pronunciation may make this argument moot. It's likely that many actors and readers will continue to opt for "Antonio."

On the CD

1. Introduction to the Sourcebooks Shakespeare
   Much Ado About Nothing: Sir Derek Jacobi

ACT 1, SCENE 1, LINES 86-107
2. Narration: Sir Derek Jacobi
3. Pauline Jameson as Beatrice and Richard Johnson as Benedick
   Living Shakespeare • 1962
4. Saskia Reeves as Beatrice and Samuel West as Benedick
   The Complete Arkangel Shakespeare • 2003

ACT 1, SCENE 1, LINES 119-150
5. Narration: Sir Derek Jacobi
6. John Horton as Benedick and Bruce Armstrong as Claudio
   CBC Radio • 1962
7. Samuel West as Benedick and Jason O'Mara as Claudio
   The Complete Arkangel Shakespeare • 2003

ACT 1, SCENE 3, LINES 1–47
8. Narration: Sir Derek Jacobi
9. Don Meyers as Conrad, David Renton as Don John, and Edwin
   Rubin as Borachio
   CBC Radio • 1962
10. Alex Lowe as Conrad, Steve Hodson as Don John, and Eddie Marsan
    as Borachio
    The Complete Arkangel Shakespeare • 2003

ACT 2, SCENE 1, LINES 230-256
11. Narration: Sir Derek Jacobi
12. Budd Knapp as Leonato, Maureen Fitzgerald as Beatrice, Bruce
    Armstrong as Claudio, and Ron Hastings as Don Pedro
    CBC Radio • 1962
13. David Bradley as Leonato, Saskia Reeves as Beatrice, Jason O'Mara
    as Claudio, and Paul Jesson as Don Pedro
    The Complete Arkangel Shakespeare • 2003

28. Alan Ayckbourn as Conrad and Peter Birrel as Borachio
    Living Shakespeare • 1962

ACT 3, SCENE 4, LINES 27–68
29. Narration: Sir Derek Jacobi
30. Faith Ward as Hero, Maureen Fitzgerald as Beatrice, and
    Flora Montgomery as Margaret
    CBC Radio • 1962
31. Abigail Docherty as Hero, Saskia Reeves as Beatrice, and
    Amanda Root as Margaret
    The Complete Arkangel Shakespeare • 2003

ACT 4, SCENE 1, LINES 248-291
32. Narration: Sir Derek Jacobi
33. John Horton as Benedick and Maureen Fitzgerald as Beatrice
    CBC Radio • 1962
34. Samuel West as Benedick and Saskia Reeves as Beatrice
    The Complete Arkangel Shakespeare • 2003

ACT 5, SCENE 1, LINES 188-220
35. Narration: Sir Derek Jacobi
36. Bruce Armstrong as Claudio, Ron Hastings as Don Pedro,
    William Fulton as Dogberry, and Edwin Rubin as Borachio
    CBC Radio • 1962
37. Robin Phillips as Claudio, Anthony Nicholls as Don Pedro,
    Colin Ellis as Dogberry, and Peter Birrel as Borachio
    Living Shakespeare • 1962

ACT 5, SCENE 2, LINES 1-29
38. Narration: Sir Derek Jacobi
39. Samuel West as Benedick and Amanda Root as Margaret
    The Complete Arkangel Shakespeare • 2003

Act 5, Scene 4, Lines 72-96

40. Narration: Sir Derek Jacobi
41. John Horton as Benedick, Maureen Fitzgerald as Beatrice, Budd Knapp as Leonato, Bruce Armstrong as Claudio, and Faith Ward as Hero
    CBC Radio • 1962
42. Richard Johnson as Benedick, Pauline Jameson as Beatrice, Newton Blick as Leonato, Robin Phillips as Claudio, and Annette Crosbie as Hero
    Living Shakespeare • 1962

43. Introduction to Speaking Shakespeare: Sir Derek Jacobi
44. Speaking Shakespeare: Andrew Wade with Santino Fontana

45. Conclusion of the Sourcebooks Shakespeare
    Much Ado About Nothing: Sir Derek Jacobi

Featured Audio Productions

The Complete Arkangel Shakespeare (2003)

Beatrice	Saskia Reeves
Benedick	Samuel West
Don Pedro	Paul Jesson
Claudio	Jason O'Mara
Hero	Abigail Docherty
Leonato	David Bradley
Margaret	Amanda Root
Dogberry	Bryan Pringle
Don John	Steve Hodson
Ursula	Sonia Ritter
Verges	Raymond Bowers
Antonio	James Greene
Balthasar	Nicholas Murchie
Borachio	Eddie Marsan
Conrad	Alex Lowe
Friar Francis	John Rogan
First Watch	Alisdair Simpson
Second Watch	Chris Pavlo
Boy	Freddie Norton

CBC Radio (1962)

Benedick	John Horton
Beatrice	Maureen Fitzgerald
Leonato	Budd Knapp
Don Pedro	Ron Hastings
Don John	David Renton
Claudio	Bruce Armstrong
Verges	Roger Crowther
Conrad	Don Meyers
Borachio	Edwin Rubin
The Messenger	Claude Bede
Friar Francis	H. Leslie Pigot
Dogberry	William Fulton
Hero	Faith Ward
Margaret	Flora Montgomery
Ursula	Phyllis Malcolm Stewart

Living Shakespeare (1962)

Leonato	Newton Blick
Messenger	Alan Ayckbourn
Beatrice	Pauline Jameson
Hero	Annette Crosbie
Don Pedro	Anthony Nicholls
Benedick	Richard Johnson
Don John	Nigel Davenport
Claudio	Robin Phillips
Borachio	Peter Birrel
Boy	Stephanie Cole
Balthazar	Christopher Keyte
Ursula	Stephanie Cole
Dogberry	Colin Ellis
Verges	John Davidson
Seacoal	Norman Tyrrell
Conrad	Alan Ayckbourn
Friar Francis	Norman Tyrrell
A Lord	Alan Ayckbourn

Sir John Gielgud Charitable Trust

Sir John Gielgud as Benedick and Dame Peggy Ashcroft as Beatrice

Note from the Series Editors

For many of us, our first and only encounter with Shakespeare was in school. We may recall that experience as a struggle, working through dense texts filled with unfamiliar words. However, those of us who were fortunate enough to have seen a play performed have altogether different memories. It may be of an interesting scene or an unusual character, but it is most likely a speech. Often, just hearing part of one instantly transports us to that time and place. "Friends, Romans, countrymen, lend me your ears," "But, soft! What light through yonder window breaks?," "To sleep, perchance to dream," "Tomorrow, and tomorrow, and tomorrow."

The Sourcebooks Shakespeare series is our attempt to use the power of performance to help you experience the play. In it, you will see photographs from various productions, on film and on stage, historical and contemporary, known worldwide or in your community. You may even recognize some actors you don't think of as Shakespearean performers. You will see set drawings, costume designs, and scene edits, all reproduced from original notes. Finally, on the enclosed audio CD, you will hear scenes from the play as performed by some of the most accomplished Shakespeareans of our times. Often, we include multiple interpretations of the same scene, showing you the remarkable richness of the text. Hear Pauline Jameson as Beatrice and Richard Johnson from the 1962 Living Shakespeare series engage in a battle of wits. Compare the same speech to the rendition by Saskia Reeves as Beatrice and Samuel West as Benedick from the 2003 Complete Arkangel Shakespeare. The actors create different worlds, different characters, different meanings.

As you read the text of the play, you can consult explanatory notes for definitions of unfamiliar words and phrases or words whose meanings have changed. These notes appear on the left pages, next to the text of the play. The audio, photographs, and other production artifacts augment the notes and they too are indexed to the appropriate lines. You can use the pictures to see how others have staged a particular scene and get ideas on costumes, scenery, blocking, and so on. As for the audio, each track represents a particular interpretation of a scene. Sometimes, a passage that's difficult to comprehend opens up when you hear it out loud. Furthermore, when you hear more than one version, you gain a keener understanding of the characters. Why did Don John act to disrupt the marriage between Claudio and Hero? Did Don Pedro and his cohorts really cause Benedick to fall in love with Beatrice? The actors made their choices and so can you. You may even come up with your own interpretation.

The text of the play, the definitions, the production notes, the audio–all of these work together, and they are included for your enjoyment. Because the audio consists of performance excerpts, it is meant to entertain. When you see a passage with an associated clip, you can read along as you hear the actors perform the scenes. Or you can sit back, close your eyes, and listen, then go back and reread the text with a new perspective. Finally, since the text is actually a script, you may find yourself reciting the lines out loud and doing your own performance!

You will undoubtedly notice that some of the audio does not exactly match the text. Also, there are photographs and facsimiles of scenes that aren't in your edition. There are many reasons for this, but foremost among them is the fact that Shakespeare scholarship continues to move forward and the prescribed ways of dealing with and interpreting text is always changing. Thus a play that was edited and published in the 1900s will be different from one published in 2006. Finally, artists have their own interpretation of the play and they too cut and change lines and scenes according to their vision.

The ways in which *Much Ado About Nothing* has been presented have varied considerably through the years. We've included essays in the book to give you glimpses into the range of the productions, showing you how other artists have approached the play and providing examples of just what changes were made and how. Courtney Lehmann writes of Kenneth Branagh's highly popular 1993 film. She discusses its exquisite Italian setting and its effect on the play. She describes the different (and uncommon) interpretations of certain characters, such as Michael Keaton's Dogberry and Imelda Staunton's Margaret. "In Production," an essay by our text editor, Jeffrey Kahan, provides an overview of how the play has been performed through the years, from Garrick/Pritchards "odd couple" portrayal in the eighteenth century to Kemble's production, which put added emphasis on the solemn parts of the play, to modern productions that set the play in places as diverse as India, a dusty Mexican village, and Neo-Napoleonic Italy. Douglas Lanier cites quite a few adaptations of the play's title in popular culture e.g., *Much Ado About Calculus* (a mathematics textbook), *Much Ado About Prom Night* (a young adult novel), and *Much Ado About Murder* (several mystery novels). Finally, for the actor in you, (and for those who want to peek behind the curtain), we have two essays that you may find especially intriguing. Andrew Wade, voice coach of the Royal Shakespeare Company for sixteen years, shares his point of view on how to understand the text and speak it. You can also listen in on him working with an actor on the opening speech of the play; perhaps you too can learn the art of speaking Shakespeare. The last essay is from an interview we conducted with each member of a cast, asking the actors about their characters and relationships. We found it fascinating to hear what they had to say on various topics; for instance, why Don John acted the way he did and whether Beatrice and Benedick lived happily ever after. The characters come to life in a way that's different from reading the book or watching a performance.

One last note: we are frequently asked why we didn't include the whole play, either in audio or video. While we enjoy the plays and are avid theatergoers, we are trying to do something more with the audio (and the production notes and the essays) than just presenting them to you. In fact, our goal is to provide you tools that will enable you to explore the play on your own, from many different directions. Our hope is that the different audio tracks, the voices of the actors, and the old production photos and notes will all engage you and illuminate the play on many levels, so that you can construct your own understanding and create your own "production," a fresh interpretation unique to you.

Though the productions we referenced and the audio clips we have included are but a miniscule sample of the play's history, we hope they encourage you to further delve into the works of Shakespeare. New editions of the play come out yearly; movie adaptations are regularly being produced; there are hundreds of theater groups in the U.S. alone; and performances could be going on right in your backyard. We echo the words of noted writer and poet Robert Graves, who said, "The remarkable thing about Shakespeare is that he is really very good—in spite of all the people who say he is very good."

We welcome you now to The Sourcebooks Shakespeare edition of *Much Ado About Nothing*.

Dominique Raccah and Marie Macaisa
Series Editors

Introduction to the Sourcebooks Shakespeare *Much Ado About Nothing*
Sir Derek Jacobi

track 1

In Production:

Much Ado About Nothing THROUGH THE YEARS

Jeffrey Kahan

ON BEATRICE AND BENEDICK

The centerpiece of any production of *Much Ado* is the battle of wills and the war of words between Benedick and Beatrice. Yet, we know surprisingly little of the original casting of the play: the performers who played Benedick or Beatrice are lost to us, though the printed text does indicate that Will Kemp and Richard Cowley played the original Dogberry and Verges. However, even for Shakespeare's contemporaries, the malapropisms of Kemp's Dogberry or Cowley's Verges were of peripheral interest: "let but *Beatrice*/And *Benedicke* be seene," wrote the poet Leonard Diggs in 1640, and "the Cockpit, Galleries, Boxes, are all full."

The recent and popular Kenneth Branagh film (1993) may suggest that the play works best when it is cast as a battle not of opposites but of equals. One of the many delights of that film derived from the knowledge that Emma Thompson and Kenneth Branagh were actually a wedded couple; we were not simply watching a Disney-esque story of a beauty who tames a beast—"In time the savage bull doth bear the yoke" (1.1.192). Indeed, one of the early comic moments of the film recalls another husband-and-wife acting team: Charles Kean played Benedick to his wife's Beatrice in 1858. The domesticity of their married life fueled a key comic moment when Ellen Tree (*nee* Ellen Kean) turned to her husband and remarked "I wonder that you will still be talking, Signor Benedick. Nobody marks you"(1.1.86-87).[i]

The comfort level necessary for this kind of acting can't be overstated, but it should be stressed that this is only one approach to the play. For much of *Much Ado*'s stage history, audiences saw the play as a prototypical "odd couple" piece. In the eighteenth century, lanky, athletic David Garrick played opposite the more portly Hannah Pritchard.

Nonetheless, the "struggle for superiority" between Pritchard's Beatrice and Garrick's Benedick was such that "the spectators could not award preference."[ii]

David Garrick as Benedick
By permission of the Folger Shakespeare Library

Early in the nineteenth century, Beatrice was played by Mrs. Dorothea Jordan, who, despite being married, was mistress to the Duke of Clarence and mother to ten of his children. She was described by William Beloe as sparkling "with vivacity, possessed a laugh and heartiness that were always inimitable, but wanted the air of good breeding."[iii] Often, she was paired with John Philip Kemble, known for his aristocratic airs. Copying this approach, American audiences were treated to the comedic pairing of the vulgar but beautiful Mrs. Morris–she enunciated badly and liked to wear shoes with heels so high that the greatest caution had to be taken that she did not pitch over during performance[iv]–who played opposite the posh, prim, and proper British actor William Hallam.

In addition to physical and character differences, the relative ages of Benedick and Beatrice have also varied. Charles Kean played the role at age sixty opposite a young Beatrice, prompting one theater critic to write that Charles Kean could no more look like Benedick than could "a dried herring."[v] Beatrice was also played by sixty-year-old Frances Abington in 1797. Abington first played Beatrice in 1775, when she was thirty-eight.

In 1836, the nineteen-year-old Helen Faucit played the part of Beatrice to Charles Kemble's sixty-one-year-old Benedick. Despite their disparate ages, their pairing was more suitable than Kemble's in 1831: his Beatrice was his own daughter, Fanny Kemble. Forty-three years later, Faucit, now sixty-three years old, reprised her role opposite the fifty-five-year-old Thomas Barry Sullivan for the opening of the Shakespeare Memorial Theatre at Stratford in 1879.

APPROACHES TO THE SCENES

Though comedy arose from the pairing of opposites, *Much Ado* was not always played for laughs. In the late eighteenth century, Benedick was played by John Philip Kemble, an actor far better known for tragedies than comedies. William Hazlitt described Kemble as "the very still-life and statuary of the stage; a perfect figure of a man; a petrifaction of sentiment, that heaves no sigh, and sheds no tear; an icicle upon the bust of Tragedy."[vi] A political and artistic traditionalist, Kemble's Shakespearean interpretations

Frances Abington as Beatrice, ca. 1785
By permission of the Folger Shakespeare Library

were aimed at curbing all rebellious tendencies and antisocial activities, including regicide and sexual license.[vii] Anxious to distance his characters from any taint of working-class vulgarity, Kemble regularly bowdlerized words: country "whoring" gave way to urbane "wenching." Even inoffensive phrases were subject to his overly severe prudery: "i' th' name of Venus" became "th' name of wonder."[viii] Offstage, Kemble lived, as it were, with "the cloak of the 'noble Roman' round him."[ix] As one praising theatergoer put it, "Who can like Kemble dignify the stage?"[x]

Dorothea Jordan
Mary Evans Picture Library

It is, therefore, not entirely surprising that Kemble's *Much Ado*, first performed on April 30, 1788, put added emphasis on the solemn nature of the play. According to Kemble's promptbook, just after Don John replies to Leonato that he is "not of many words, but I thank you," Leonato leads Don Pedro and the others off stage. Before leaving, Beatrice, played first by Elizabeth Farren (and later, in the 1790s, by Dorothea Jordan) offers Benedick her hand, which he refuses to kiss. This sullen Benedick, it seems, is in many

John Philip Kemble
Mary Evans Picture Library

ways darker than Don John, who, while not of many words, has–at least to this early point in the play–been civil enough. Perhaps worse yet, Benedick, despite a text that singles him out as a war hero, seems rather cowardly. When Beatrice teases Benedick by calling him the "prince's jester," Kemble walks about "very much vexed... till, at last, he runs away... and she after him... ."

To this point in the play, the audience's sympathies are clearly with Beatrice, and, like Beatrice, they must be turned. In Act 4, Kemble's Benedick shows that, while he may dislike Beatrice, he is in many ways the only noble character in the play. When Hero faints in the church, it is Kemble who, from her left, rushes forward to catch her fall, while Beatrice braces her from the right. Visually, then, our lovers' first embrace is in their support of Hero. When she regains her footing, Beatrice and Benedick hug each other and weep. Moments later, alone with Beatrice, Kemble expands the close of the scene to reaffirm Benedick's military prowess and his honorable love of Beatrice:

BENEDICK

Enough; I am engaged; I'll challenge him.

BEATRICE

Will you?

BENEDICK

Upon my soul, I will. I'll kiss your hand, and so leave you. [*Kisses her hand.*] By this hand, Claudio shall render me a dear account.

BEATRICE

You'll be sure to challenge him.

BENEDICK

By those bright eyes, I will.

BEATRICE

My dear friend, kiss my hand again. [*He kisses her hand.*]

BENEDICK

As you hear of me, so think of me. Go comfort your cousin: I must say, she is dead:–and so, farewell.

Both going.

BEATRICE

Benedick,–kill him; kill him, if you can.

BENEDICK

As sure as he is alive, I will.

Beatrice's reiteration to "kill him; kill him" underscores that, while she may be a woman, she's far more ferocious than her masculine counterparts. But it is her closing "if you can" which perhaps carries more consequence. Benedick is not playing a game here. This Claudio is a proven and battle-hardened combatant, and Benedick has now promised to exchange far more than foul words with him. In keeping with the somber nature of this version, the lines after Benedick's challenge, including Pedro and Claudio's exchange that Benedick's wits have been unbalanced by his love of Beatrice (5.1.177-178), are duly excised, as is his exchange in 5.2 with Margaret. That exchange suggested that Benedick was aware of, and not immune from, Margaret's sexual allure and that he enjoyed a bit of sordid wordplay. In an effort to remain beloved of all the ladies, Kemble cut the passage to render it more decorous than licentious:

MARGARET

Will you then write me a sonnet in praise of my beauty?

BENEDICK

In so high a style Margaret, that no man living shall come over it; for, in most comely truth, thou deservest it, and so I pray thee, call Beatrice.

MARGARET

Well, I will call Beatrice to you.

Exit Margaret.

Compare that to the original text he used:

MARGARET

Will you then write me a sonnet in praise of my beauty?

BENEDICK

In so high a style Margaret, that no man living shall come over it, for, in most comely truth, thou deservest it.

MARGARET

To have no man come over me?   Why, shall I always keep below stairs?

BENEDICK

Thy wit is as quick as the greyhound's mouth: it catches.

MARGARET

And yours, as blunt as the fencer's foils, which hit, but hurt not.

BENEDICK

A most manly wit Margaret; it will not hurt a woman. And so I pray thee, call Beatrice. I give thee the bucklers.

MARGARET

Give us the swords. We have bucklers of our own.

BENEDICK

If you use them, Margaret, you must put in the pikes with a vice, and they are dangerous weapons for maids.

MARGARET

Well, I will call Beatrice to you, who, I think, hath legs.

Exit Margaret

Another deletion completes Benedick's reformation, one that might surprise readers. Whereas in Shakespeare's original Don John is taken prisoner, prompting Benedick to promise that he will, on his wedding night, be preoccupied with the devising of "brave punishments" to be practiced upon Don Pedro's brother, Kemble cuts the exchange altogether. Don John is forgotten, if not forgiven; our attention remains focused on Benedick, the married man, who becomes the jester:

BENEDICK
> Prince thou art sad.

DON PEDRO
> Yes, I've got a tooth-ake.

BENEDICK
> Got the tooth-ake!– Get thee a wife; and all will be well.–Nay, laugh not, laugh not:–Your jibes and mockeries I laugh to scorn; no staff more reverend than one tipp'd with horn.

Not exactly a thigh-slapper, but it does suggest that Benedick has become a far more jovial creature than the single, if not solitary, sourpuss we took him to be.

SETTING AND COSTUMES

Just as the characterizations of Beatrice and Benedick have varied, so too there have been differenthave the stagings of the play throughout the years. Though *Much Ado* is set in Messina, Italy, just after a war, in Charles Kean's 1858 production at the Princess's Theatre, the war has done little damage to the city. Audiences were treated to a sunset view of the port of Messina, the sun gradually disappearing in the west, casting its declining rays on the houses and the ships. Then the moon rose on a brilliant masquerade scene with variegated lights from garden and bridge lamps that shone through the arches of the palace. The church scene (4.1) for Henry Irving's 1882 Lyceum production featured an Italian cathedral with stained-glass windows and statues of saints, thirty-foot-high pillars, and a canopied roof of crimson plush from which hung golden lamps. The floor was covered with vases of flowers, and flaming candles rose to a height of eighteen feet.[xi]

Not all companies opted for the traditional or the picturesque. The set for Edward Gordon Craig's 1903-04 production relied more on nuances of lighting. For the church scene, Craig did away with Irving's formality in favor of a pool of colored light, which appeared to have been cast through a stained-glass window onto the stage below.

Other productions used lavish costumes to reset the scene. John Barton's RSC production (1976)–in retrospect, a star-studded affair with Judi Dench as Beatrice and Donald Sinden as Benedick–set the play in India during the reign of the British Raj. Leonato, Don Pedro, Claudio, Don John, and Benedick all wore traditional British military garb,; Dogberry and the Watch were accoutered as turbaned Sikhs.

The Illinois Shakespeare Festival (1998) set the play in a dusty Mexican village; in the New York City Spartan Theater production of the play (2002), the men wore suits, not tights, and Dogberry proudly paraded in Boy Scout attire. Beatrice sported a "boyz r stupid" tee shirt, while the noblemen discussed love in their New Balance sneakers over a round of golf.[xii] In a 2002 Pittsburgh production, the Off-Tryon Theatre Company opted for a hybrid of Thai pantaloons and Asian silk jackets.[xiii] Likewise, in the RSC's 2002 production, Harriet Walter's Beatrice was more comfortable in pants straddling a motorcycle than sashaying demurely in a dress.

John Woodvine as Dogberry along with the watch in the 1976 RSC production directed by John Barton
Photographer Reg Wilson © Royal Shakespeare Company

The 1958 RSC production of *Much Ado* set the play in a sort of Neo-Napoleonic Italy, the women in tight-laced dresses, twirling crinoline parasols; the men in French flowered waistcoats and tasseled smoking caps. Three years later, the RSC set the play in a Jane Austen-style Regency. Combining the two, the Branagh film is set and dressed in a seemingly timeless or vaguely eighteenth-century Italy; "a never-never land of eternal present or mixed into a kind of Euromulch."[xiv] A kind of Euro-Disney may be more accurate: as the film opens, a group of tanned, well-fed men and women are picnicking and amusing themselves with song and poetry. Considering that there is a war underway not far off, their Arcadian delights seem odd; but we soon learn that the war is of little consequence, and none of any name have been killed in action. When the heroes return, none seem to have suffered very much. Their milk-white jackets are neither war-torn nor bloodstained. Even when Benedick later challenges Claudio to a duel, the tension of the imminent fight is deflated when we learn that the worse that can happen is that Claudio will be subscribed a coward. In a world where sticks and stones (or even swords and cannonballs) do not break bones, we can hardly expect words, even foul words, to hurt very much. When Benedick promises "brave punishments" (5.4.120) for Don John, we're less inclined to imagine the villain being broken on the rack as his being given a stern reprimand and perhaps barred from picnicking with the gang for at least a month.

The film works best not when Branagh and Thompson coo like lovebirds, but when they sting each other like angry wasps, or, as in this scene, engage in fast and furious one-upmanship:

BENEDICK
  They swore that you were almost sick for me.
BEATRICE
  They swore that you were well-nigh dead for me.

(5.4.80-81)

While some critics dismissed the film—most notably Peter Travers of *Rolling Stone*, who asserted that the movie carries the emotional wallop of an episode of *Beverly Hills, 90210* (an American soap opera about a group of rich teenagers)—Branagh's film remains, like Shakespeare's original, a worthy fan favorite.[xv]

CONCLUSION

The various productions of *Much Ado About Nothing* throughout the years demonstrate that the characters of Beatrice and Benedick, and their relationship, encourage exploration in different contexts. Whether Benedick is sixty years old to Beatrice's nineteen or whether it is Beatrice who is sixty, be they in India during the reign of the British Raj or in a dusty Mexican village, their enduring appeal connects with and entertains audiences everywhere.

ENDNOTES

[i] Charles E. L. Wingate, Shakespeare's Heroines on the Stage. (New York: Thomas Y. Crowell & Company, 1895), 48.

[ii] Ibid., 35-6.

[iii] Ibid., 42.

[iv] Ibid., 51.

[v] Ibid., 49.

[vi] William Hazlitt, The Complete Works of William Hazlitt in Twenty-one Volumes, ed. P. P. Howe. (London and Tornoto: J. M. Dent and Sons, 1930), V:304.

[vii] James Boaden, Memoirs of John Philip Kemble, I:92-3.

viii Herschel Baker, John Philip Kemble: The Actor in His Theatre (Cambridge, MA: Harvard University Press, 1942), 115.

ix Linda Kelly, The Kemble Era: John Philip Kemble, Sarah Siddons and the London Stage (New York: Random House, 1980), 103.

x Actors and Editors, A Poem By an Undergraduate (London: W. Smith and Co., 1817), 33.

xi Laurence Irving, quoted in A.R. Humphreys, Much Ado About Nothing, 40.

xii See Nina Judar's review. Show Business Online. http://www.showbusinessweekly.com/archive/133/much-ado-about-nothing.html

xiii See Lynn Trenning's review for ArtSavant. http://artsavant.com/reviews/2002lmt1114.html.

xiv Alison Light, 'The Importance of Being Ordinary,' Sight and Sound 3.9 (1993), 16-19.

xv Peter Travers, 'Much About About Nothing' – Review. http://www.rollingstone.com/reviews/movie/_/id/5949003?rnd=1143048855800&has-player=true&version=6.0.12.1483

As Performed

By the cast of the Kenneth Branagh film at Villa Vignamaggio, Tuscany, Italy in 1993

Courtney Lehmann

Shortly before its U.S. release on May 7, 1993, Kenneth Branagh's film adaptation of *Much Ado About Nothing* was screened at the Shakespeare Association of America meeting in Atlanta. Then just a first-year graduate student, I remember well the account of the film offered by the Shakespeare scholar leading our class as he sauntered in, fresh off the plane, and proclaimed: "True to its title, the film was indeed much ado about *nothing*." Although he chortled on about leather pants and men on horseback in a mildly bemused tone, his contempt was clear. Nearly two years later I screened *Much Ado About Nothing* for my sister, a recent college graduate and an avid reader of historical fiction. I watched her facial expressions throughout the film, anxiously seeking her approval of the production and, more importantly, of the 400-year-old playwright around whom my life's work seemed destined to revolve. She laughed at Benedick and cried for Hero and, following the film's euphoric ending, she resolved to go directly to Barnes and Noble to "buy the book." With one foot out the door, she turned to me and asked: "By the way, who wrote it?"

With the exception of his debut film, *Henry V* (1989), which received multiple Oscar nominations and enjoyed virtually unanimous praise, Kenneth Branagh's Shakespeare films have been the subject of a distinctly polarized reception. As the above anecdote illustrates, public opinion typically fractures along scholarly and popular lines; whereas academic audiences tend to deplore Branagh as often as they applaud him, mass audiences are generally more appreciative of his user-friendly approach to adaptation. For my part, when I study *Much Ado About Nothing*, I am critical of what I perceive to be Branagh's social conservatism–a point to which I will return. However, when I watch the film with my glasses off, I share the giddiness of the performers themselves, who never fail to transport me into their Tuscan fairy

The cast of Branagh's 1993 film: Michael Keaton (Dogberry), Rober Sean Leonard (Claudio), Keanu Reeves (Don John), Kate Beckinsale (Hero), Emma Thompson (Beatrice), Kenneth Branagh (Benedick), and Denzel Washington (Don Pedro).
<cred>Courtesy: Douglas Lanier

tale. Hence, when, in the course of an interview at an international confer-ence, I was asked what my favorite Shakespeare film was, I impulsively blurted: "Kenneth Branagh's *Much Ado about Nothing*!" Then I glanced down at the list that my colleagues had generated, quickly noting that Branagh's name was nowhere to be found. Rather, I saw Olivier, Kozintsev, Welles, and Kurosawa, "the big four" auteurs whose work has become the standard by which all Shakespeare films are, at least implicitly, evaluated. An untenured professor at the time, I was convinced that I had sabotaged my entire career. How could I have been so naïve as to think that the interviewer wanted to know which Shakespeare film I most enjoyed watching–for enter-tainment–rather than the film that I found most fruitful for analysis? The more I thought about it, however, the more I realized that given a second chance, my answer would have been exactly the same.

SHAKESPEARE WITH A VIEW

In "The Making of" featurette included in the most recent DVD version of *Much Ado About Nothing*, Branagh explains that Shakespeare is best approached not as a figure of worship but as a worthy adversary, whose plays demand a "blood and guts, passionate" style of performance that is "emotionally fearless" and, at times, even "emotionally reckless." Branagh's *Much Ado* is a film in which passion becomes a veritable production value, courtesy of the exquisite Italian shooting locations that make romantic scenery synonymous with rapturous sentiments. Whereas Branagh's other films rely on studios, sets, and landscapes based entirely in England to recreate their Shakespearean settings, this adaptation, according to Branagh, demands travel directly to Italy, where *Much Ado*'s "hot-tempered Italianate qualities" emerge in bold relief against the subdued "'Englishness' of the other plays" (*Screenplay,* ix).

In whisking Shakespeare away from colder English climates and cultural inclinations for an Italian holiday, Branagh inserts his adaptation into both Renaissance tradition and cinematic trends. In Shakespeare's own day, Italy was the place where well-to-do English families sent boys to become men, based on the belief that the country's warm nights and welcoming natives would indulge and, subsequently, exorcise the intemperate urges of youth, enabling the aspiring gentlemen to return home prepared for the serious business of adulthood. That Italy retains this power to prevail over repression and release inhibitions is evident in Emma Thompson's remarks on the set of the film, shot during the dog days of August: "To be here is so incredible," she exclaims, breathily. "Suddenly these kinds of great passions burst out of people. And to do it [the film], and to be here, in this heat, where you're panting and sweating, is fantastic." Thompson could just as easily be describing the highly successful Merchant/Ivory film to which *Much Ado* is indebted, namely, *A Room with a View* (1985), which takes the English experience of Italy–and its sublimely liberating effects–for theme. Significantly, two other films devoted to the same theme, *Where Angels Fear to Tread* (Charles Sturridge, 1991) and *Enchanted April* (Mike Newell, 1992),

immediately preceded the release of *Much Ado*. Since then, the "Italian vaca-
tion" film has become a mini-genre in its own right, casting its nets beyond
England to explore the country's felicitous influence on a desperate house-
wife in *Bread and Tulips* (Silvio Soldini, 2000), depressed Danes in *Italian for
Beginners* (Lone Scherfig, 2000), and an American divorcé in *Under the Tuscan Sun* (Audrey Wells, 2003). Seeking to capitalize on this escapist trend,
Branagh's film features an open-air, all-male bathing scene in its opening
credit sequence, conspicuously alluding to the *al fresco* lake antics in *A Room
with a View* and, of course, the theme of rebirth under Italian skies.

One thing oddly out of place in *Much Ado*'s meticulously constructed,
Mediterranean mise-en-scene is Branagh's own entry into the film, which
immediately precedes this playful moment of cinematic intertextuality.
Eager to convey the tangible virility of Don Pedro's men as they spur their
steeds toward Leonato's villa, Branagh describes their approach as a swirl of
"heat haze and dust, grapes and horseflesh" and, he adds, "a nod to *The Magnificent Seven*" (*Screenplay,* viii). Given the great number of spaghetti westerns that emerged from the same era as this iconic film, why does Branagh
suddenly shift terrain from Tuscan outback to American frontier? It is
almost as if, for just a moment, the Italian heat becomes too much for him
and he falls back on the familiar—in this case, the patented formulas of Hol-
lywood. Indeed, *Much Ado*'s Italian environs unleash an "emotional reck-
lessness" to which not even Branagh is immune, becoming the source of
everything—in the words of Sergio Leone—that is "good, bad, and ugly" in
this film.

THE "GOOD"

Like the entreaties of the Chorus in *Henry V, Much Ado* implores the audience to summon its "imaginary forces" to move not just men but also moun-
tains, for Branagh's film transports the city of Messina itself across the
"perilous narrow ocean" (*Henry V,* Pro. 18, 22) that separates Sicily from the
Italian mainland in order to shoot on location in Chianti country. Although
the name of Messina is retained, the undulating splendor of the Tuscan countryside is unmistakable as we enter the film through Leonato's painting of his
villa. Panning away from the canvas to the real Villa Vignamaggio, the camera pauses to frame this otherwordly place nestled amid groves of cypress

trees. So beautiful is this image that the audience is led to wonder if it has fallen for another *tromp l'oeil* effect, for surely no one really *lives* in this unspoiled paradise. Before we can linger too long in our surmise, Leonato intrudes upon the static shot, paint brush in hand, to expose a foreground peopled with picnickers—bare-chested men and buxom women who indulge each other in the abundant supply of home-grown wine, cheese, grapes, and breads—creating an extravagant pastoral idyll more reminiscent of Ben Johnson's ode "To Penshurst" than anything in Shakespeare's play.

In fact, the entire opening sequence of Branagh's *Much Ado* has *nothing* to do with Shakespeare's play, which begins on a decidedly darker note. Following the news of Don Pedro's arrival from the wars, Leonato asks the herald: "How many gentlemen have you lost in this action?" (1.1.5). The messenger's curt reply: "But few of any sort, and none of name" (1.1.6), is indicative of the straightforward hierarchies that governed Renaissance culture, wherein lives were valued according to parentage and property, not merit. Such discriminatory statements are common in the Shakespeare

Emma Thompson as Beatrice, Kate Beckinsale as Hero, and the citizens of Messina on the way to a picnic. © Sygma/Corbis

canon, but they sit far less comfortably with Branagh, who frequently cites his working-class background as the source of his desire to make films "for the masses." Quite masterfully, Branagh's seemingly audacious decision to relocate Messina to the very heart of Chianti country offers a temporary solution to this recurring problem.

On an aesthetic level alone, the blunt prose with which Shakespeare's play starts is no match for the visual poetry of the film's picnicking tableau, a bravura beginning which, Branagh explains, is modeled on an "Impressionist painting" (*Screenplay*, 6). Offering more than just an aesthetic frame of reference, Impressionism also points to *Much Ado*'s ideological underpinnings. Distinguished not only by an interest in the effects of natural lighting but also by a preoccupation with artificial social structures like class, the Impressionist movement gave rise to utopian sentiments, based on its depiction of public places as sites of potentially serendipitous interactions among heterogeneous peoples. Unlike the industrialized landscape of the real Messina, Chianti country fosters a utopian sensibility as a place where people converge to consume rather than to produce, a place where it seems as though all the labor is undertaken by nature itself—by this "magical landscape of vines and olives that seems untouched by much of modern life"—in Branagh's apt phrasing (*Screenplay*, xiv). Long before we hear the insulting opening exchange between Leonato and the messenger, then, we have already derived our prevailing "impression" of Branagh's Messina as a place where languid bodies and lilting umbrellas indicate that labor and, consequently, the social divisions on which it is based, are irrelevant.

The "Bad"

Significantly, the imaginary migration that *Much Ado* undertakes from Sicilian outpost to Tuscan center mirrors Branagh's real move from Irish nobody to English superstar. Seeking to escape the surging sectarian violence of the Troubles, Branagh's family fled the war-torn city of Belfast to settle in English suburbia. Upon arrival, however, they discovered that "it was not a good time to be Irish" there either (Branagh, *Beginning*, 23). "Many of the children at school had older brothers in the Army," Branagh recalls in his autobiography. "Every death reported on the television news made me try to change even further; I longed just to blend in. After a year or so I'd managed to become English at school and remain Irish at home" (23). But the stress of this acting routine proved unbearable and, before long, Branagh found himself abandoning his "double life" (24) to become entirely English, as his voice "gradually took on the twang of suburbia" (24). The new part suited him exceedingly well, affirmation of which came in the form of acceptance to the Royal Academy of Dramatic Art in London, leading roles at the Royal Shakespeare Company and, eventually, enough clout to start his own theater and film company, appropriately named "Renaissance." Like Shakespeare, whose success in the theater entitled his father, a mere glover, to a gentleman's coat-of-arms, Branagh's performances—first in life and then in art— retroactively earned him an English pedigree.

Whatever feelings remain from this "traumatic period" in which his "whole family was undergoing an enforced change of personality" (23), Branagh never voices them, for to do so would be quite literally out of character. But *other* characters or, better put, characters who become "others" in his films, as targets of a peculiar representational violence that is incommensurate with their crimes, suggest how precipitously the repressed can rise to the surface, particularly in the intense heat of the Tuscan sun. In *Much Ado*, these instances of representational violence are triggered by acts of betrayal, intimating the ambivalence with which Branagh regards his own decision to turn his back on Ireland, as well as the opportunities that cinema presents for projecting his Troubles onto others.

In the meantime, let me be that I am, and seek not to alter me.

(1.3.27)

According to the Renaissance system of primogeniture, being a second-born son meant a life of few options, often limited to a future in the church. Being born a bastard, however, was a complete dead end, for these figures of disputed paternity were not even worthy of inscription in the parish birth register. Once a child torn between an Irish birthright and English aspirations, Branagh would seem disposed to sympathize with characters like *Much Ado*'s Don John but, in fact, he subjects Don John to further marginalization, representing him as a figure whose evil is motivated less by his bastardy than by his repressed homosexuality. Even before we encounter Don

John alone with his distinctly unmerry men, his aberrance is encoded in his lodging; unlike the others who are housed in the bright upper stories of the villa, he is stowed away in a subterranean bedchamber, the darkness of which is punctuated only by an eerie red glow, suggestive of a "hot-tempered" desire that requires hiding. That Don John is not merely aberrant but, more specifically, sexually deviant is apparent from our first glimpse of him in his quarters, where he lies face down and oiled up on a stone slab, enjoying a massage from Conrade. When Don John rises from his prone position, relishing his sullen disposition and sinister plans, he pauses at various junctures to clutch Conrade's face and body in ways that intertwine the behavior of lovers with the plotting of criminals.

This reading of Don John's character leads to the socially conservative conclusion that he thwarts Claudio's marriage to Hero because he is a traitor to normative sexual desire, that is, to the heterosexual unions which, in the Renaissance, were central to the maintenance of social order and geopolitical alliances. In Douglas Greene's terms, Don John is a "queer traitor," someone who elides the distinction between personal homosexuality and political treason—a figure who, significantly, appears in all of Branagh's Shakespeare films–from Scroop in *Henry V* to Osric in *Hamlet* and Boyet in *Love's Labour's Lost*. Referring to himself as "a plain-dealing villain," Don John tells us that "I cannot hide what I am" (1.3.9), but Branagh is nevertheless compelled to endow him with a double life as a homosexual. What better analogy for his own painful past as a "closeted" Irishman?

THE "UGLY"

Although women in the English Renaissance made it into the birth registers, they enjoyed fewer privileges than bastards, for their flesh was officially owned by their nearest male kin: father, brother, husband, or even son. In Branagh's film, Hero's waiting woman, Margaret, becomes Don John's unofficial partner in crime as a figure who is also sexually deviant—in this case, promiscuous—representing another "hot-blooded" behavior which, like homosexuality, has the potential to destabilize the social order. Recognizing that the audience would not be familiar with the Renaissance conception of female speech as a sign of sexual availability, Branagh alters the play's offstage account of Margaret "talking to a man" at Hero's window (the bait that

Don John uses to persuade Claudio that his fiancé is unchaste) by showing Margaret actually engaging in sexual intercourse. Framed in a fashion similar to Don John in his chamber, Margaret's bare back is exposed to the spectator through the window above the courtyard where Don John, Claudio, and Don Pedro gather; her dark hair, nearly identical to Hero's, falls in ringlets beyond her shoulders, bouncing and jostling with each of Borachio's standing thrusts, as he murmurs—for the benefit of the audience below— "Hero. Hero. Hero." By actually showing a scene that is merely described in the play Branagh succeeds in making "Hero's" deception of Claudio more believable for modern audiences, but he also makes Claudio's ensuing misogyny against her more acceptable. Indeed, as witnesses to the crime, we are prepared to privilege what we have seen over what we know to be true, having just watched Claudio watch "Hero" engage in the act which, Don Pedro is quick to allege, she has committed "a thousand times in secret" (4.1.88).

But the real upshot of this directorial decision is the vilification of Margaret. In Shakespeare's play, Margaret is cleared of any premeditated wrong, as Borachio assures Leonato that she "knew not what she did when she spoke to me / But always hath been just and virtuous" (5.1.266-267). Our inclination to believe this statement stems partly from the fact that Margaret's chastity is not explicitly compromised in Shakespeare's play, for even in the Renaissance, sometimes talk is *just talk*. Branagh, however, not only exposes Margaret as a whore but also implicates her as a traitor to her sex at Hero's wedding. When Claudio begins to physically and verbally abuse Hero for the events of the preceding night, harping on the question "What man was he talked with you yesternight / Out at your window betwixt twelve and one?" (4.1.77-78), the camera cuts to Margaret's shocked expression as she puts two and two together. This reaction shot has no basis in Shakespeare's play, which does not specify Margaret's presence at the wedding, let alone her awareness of the plot into which she has been sewn. In Branagh's film, however, her moment of recognition and ensuing silence lends credibility to the old adage that "women are their own worst enemies," rather than placing blame at the door of a pathological patriarchy that regards women's bodies as male property.

> O, what men dare do! What they may do;
> what they daily do, not knowing what they do!

> (4.1.14-15)

Not even Emma Thompson's stunning performance as Beatrice, whose every word seems to better the one before it, can balance the weight of these combined imputations against the female sex. Thompson is the indisputable star of the film—giddy, vulnerable, crazed—and uncannily capable of wrenching tears from the audience in each case. When Don Pedro says to her, smiling, "to be merry best becomes you; for, out of question, you were born in a merry hour" (2.1.253-254), Thompson locks eyes with him and replies with sudden sobriety: "No, sure, my lord, my mother cried; but then there was a star danced, and under that was I born" (2.1.255-256). Exquisitely guarded, Beatrice never lets us get too close to her; hence, in the very next breath, she throws her arms in the air, shouting ecstatically: "Cousins, God give you joy!" (2.1.256). Even more breathtaking are the undertones of female solidarity she consistently extracts from Shakespeare's play—particularly in the chapel scene where, following her quiet confession of love for Benedick, she utters a vow that is dearer still. Desperate to avenge Claudio's slander of her cousin, she turns suddenly rabid and screams: "O God, that I were a man! I would eat his heart in the market place" (4.1.290-291). It seems hardly coincidental that Branagh's Benedick should play the protofeminist at this precise moment, taking up Beatrice's challenge and vowing to kill Claudio, his brother-in-arms. Ultimately, though, neither Beatrice's brilliance nor Benedick's chivalry prove a sufficient distraction from Branagh's ugly treatment of Margaret who, unlike her Shakespearean sister, has the power to redeem Hero but chooses not to exercise it.

THE END
Branagh signals the beginning, middle, and end of the film with aural rather than visual cues, as Patrick Doyle's arrangement of the song "Sigh No More, Ladies" functions as a kind of Chorus, repeating the ironic moral that "*Men* are constant never." In so doing, the film ultimately halts the misogynistic momentum of a play that begins with a degrading pun on the female genitalia as "nothing" or "no *thing*" and ends with Benedick's allusion to cuckold's horns—the mark of an unfaithful wife—in his playful imperative to Don Pedro: "Prince, thou art sad; get thee a wife, get thee a wife: there is no staff more reverend than one tipped with horn" (5.4.115-117). Wisely, Branagh cuts this inauspicious phrase and ends the line with the repetition

of Benedick's challenge to "get thee a wife." In so doing, however, he inadvertently draws attention to the fact that Don Pedro, played by the only actor of color in the entire cast, is also the only character who remains unmatched at the film's conclusion. Literally lacking a partner, Don Pedro does not join in the magnificent, operatic reprise of "Sigh No More" that accompanies all the newlyweds, family, and friends as they clasp hands to dance us out of the film. Of all the performance decisions that Branagh makes in adapting *Much Ado* to the screen, this one is the most peculiar, for it creates an insurmountable barrier to what is otherwise one of the most satisfying, *truly* happy endings in all of filmed Shakespeare. Branagh has never offered an adequate explanation for this decision, sometimes claiming that it was Washington's choice, other times attributing it to an incidental effect of blocking, and still other times suggesting that the camera, anxious to crane higher and higher above the festivities, simply loses sight of the film's highest ranking character. But in light of Washington's commanding presence throughout the film, his conspicuous absence at the end is impossible to ignore. Although Branagh admits in his final stage directions that "we note the melancholic,

Judi Dench as Beatrice and Donald Sinden as Benedick in the 1977 RSC production.
Photo: Donald Cooper

solitary figure of Don Pedro," both he–and the camera–quickly move on "to catch the afternoon sun, the sounds of happiness floating on the air, and a breathtaking view of [the] fairy tale countryside" (*Screenplay,* 83). In his haste to escape the coming darkness, Branagh misses the shadow of his own past, which he casts onto the *only* character in his film who, try as he might, will never "just blend in" to this all-white Tuscan fairy tale.

The 1988 theatrical version of *Much Ado* that inspired Branagh's film was a production directed by Dame Judi Dench, who was determined to stress "the dark side" of Shakespeare's play. Although Dench recognized the levity that the comedy demanded in places, it was the play's "strange treatment of sex, and its often sinister quality" that she most "wanted to underline" (*Beginning,* 202).

Five years later, Branagh's film would take the opposite tack, equally committed to approaching *Much Ado* sunny side up. It seems only fitting, then, that the film role for which Branagh is, at least currently, best known is his performance as Professor Gilderoy Lockhart, teacher of Defense Against the Dark Arts in *Harry Potter and the Chamber of Secrets* (Chris Columbus, 2002). Cinema is, of course, a constitutively dark art that emerges from the projection of light through a series of photographic negatives, and in this respect alone Branagh has his work cut out for him in seeking to defend us from the dark side of Shakespeare's plays.

I love Kenneth Branagh's *Much Ado About Nothing* for the same ten things I hate about it. And this ambivalence is precisely what Branagh's films, and Shakespeare's plays–and, of course, Sergio Leone's spaghetti westerns—are all about: they hold the mirror up to *our* nature, and they keep it there, until we see the good, the bad, and the ugly. In spite of itself, then, *Much Ado About Nothing* is a fairy tale that is true to life.

Works Cited

(1) Kenneth Branagh, *Beginning* (St. Martin's Press, 1989).
(2) Kenneth Branagh, *Much Ado About Nothing by William Shakespeare. Screenplay, Introduction, and Notes on the Making of the Movie* (W. W. Norton and Co., 1993).

"A Kind of Merry War"

Much Ado About Nothing IN POPULAR CULTURE

Douglas Lanier

Much Ado About Nothing has long been a dependable staple of the Shakespearean stage repertory, but it has not been particularly favored by modern popular culture for adaptation or citation. This has not always been the case. In 1662, William Davenant, member of one of two companies licensed by the king to perform plays, combined *Much Ado* with elements from *Measure from Measure* to create *The Law Against Lovers*, the first adaptation of Shakespeare performed on the public stage after the restoration of Charles II. When Samuel Pepys, indefatigable diarist of the period, saw the work, he pronounced it "a good play and well performed." Even though Shakespeare's original script for *Much Ado* was performed as early as 1721, the tradition of amalgamating *Much Ado* with other plays continued well into the eighteenth century. Charles Johnson's *Love in a Forest* (1723), a version of *As You Like It*, assigns some of Benedick's lines to Jaques as he falls in love with Celia; in *The Universal Passion*, James Miller dovetailed *Much Ado* with Moliére's *La Princesse D'Elide*. However, since the eighteenth century, there have been few adaptations of *Much Ado*, especially when compared to other Shakespearean comedies of its stature such as *A Midsummer Night's Dream* or *Twelfth Night*.

Contemporary adaptations do exist. *Much Ado* was updated as part of the BBC's *Shakespeare Re-Told* series in 2005, the play's action transposed to a fictional TV news studio. Beatrice and Benedick are re-imagined as bickering anchors, and Claudio and Hero as Claude and Hero, a sportscaster and weathergirl whose impending marriage Don, a jealous videographer, schemes to destroy. One of the few modern novels to take up *Much Ado* is Joan Silsby's *The Devil's Bride* (2005), a sequel to *Much Ado About Nothing* that focuses on the punishment of Don John. Forced to redeem himself by wooing and winning Benedick's sister Lady Allegra, Don John learns that because of a gypsy's curse, Allegra's last three suitors died before they could

marry her. The novel has recently been adapted for the stage and will be produced in fall 2006. For the most part, however, popular adaptations of *Much
Ado* are few and far between.

There are several reasons why modern adaptors have not followed in the
footsteps of their eighteenth-century forebears. *Much Ado*'s comedy is driven
to a great extent by wordplay that is rather culturally specific and thus resists
easy transposition into contemporary genres. To modern audiences the plot's
concern with male honor and female chastity seems excessive and outdated,
especially in the aborted wedding scene; conventions of courtship that might
accord with eighteenth- and even nineteenth-century notions of propriety and
virtue have become increasingly difficult to square with more sexually liber-
ated styles of twentieth-century romance. As enduringly appealing as the
bickering lovers Benedick and Beatrice and the bumbling Dogberry might be,
the Claudio and Hero plotline has limited the play's appeal to modern adaptors. Most important, the play features no grand speeches or descriptive passages that seem ripe for citation or parody, nor readily recognizable iconic
moments like *Romeo and Juliet*'s balcony scene, Hamlet's graveyard address
to Yorick's skull, or Lear's raging on the heath–to which to allude.

"NOTES, NOTES, FORSOOTH AND NOTHING": *Much Ado* AND MUSIC

Even so, *Much Ado* has exerted modest influence in contemporary popular
culture and served as the source for a number of works. Perhaps prompted
by the musical pun on "noting" in the play's title, recrafting of *Much Ado* to
musical form has been a favored adaptation strategy. Central to these musical adaptations–and indicative of the play's interpretation after the advent
of the Romantic movement–is Hector Berlioz's 1862 opera *Béatrice et
Bénédick*. As the title indicates, Berlioz refocused Shakespeare's plot on the
passionate *sturm und drang* of the tempestuous lovers, making them the
comic equivalent of Romeo and Juliet (whom Berlioz had earlier portrayed
in musical form in an 1839 tone poem). In the libretto to *Béatrice et
Bénédick*, Berlioz's own reshaping of Shakespeare's text, he jettisons Don
John's besmirching of Hero's character and adds a comic subplot involving
an inept choirmaster–the musical equivalent of Dogberry–hired to direct the
music for Claudio and Hero's wedding. In this version Hero and Claudio's
marriage is never in doubt, and preparations for it become the backdrop for

their friends' playful engineering of Beatrice and Benedick's courtship. The operatic version by British composer Sir Charles Villiers Stanford, produced in 1900, is far more faithful to Shakespeare's script. Stanford includes the plot to ruin Hero's reputation, as well as Dogberry and Seacole who, in this version, reveal Don John's treachery and save the day. Stanford's adaptation was of a piece with efforts in his later career to create operas based on English and Irish sources. Though his *Much Ado About Nothing* was not successful in its initial British premiere, it has since been performed with some regularity and is valued for its ensemble work and charming romantic passages. Also notable is the operatic adaptation by Tikhon Khrennikov, *Mnogo shuma ... iz_za serdets* [*Much Ado about Hearts*, 1972], one of several comic operettas by the noted Soviet composer, as well as an appealing orchestral suite on *Much Ado About Nothing* by American composer Erich Korngold. Korngold's suite, an entirely instrumental piece, has been regularly recorded.

Much Ado has also served as the basis for a handful of popular musicals. Hy Conrad's *Ta-Dah!*, a modern musical loosely based on Shakespeare's play, made a brief appearance in an off-Broadway production in 1978. Creator of several musicals based upon literary classics, British composer Bernard Taylor, inspired by Kenneth Branagh's film of the play, produced *Much Ado* in 1997 (with a cast recording appearing in 1998); Taylor's lively mix of pseudo-Elizabethan music with Broadway-style songs sought to blend period and contemporary styles in a novel way. In a very different vein, The Troubadour Theater, a Los Angeles-based troupe specializing in Shakespeare musical hybrids, has produced *Much Adoobie Brothers About Nothing* (2006), a modern Shakespearean burlesque that combines the plot of *Much Ado* with rewritten versions of tunes by the Doobie Brothers, the 70s rock band.

More substantial are two recent productions that, while strictly speaking not musicals, nevertheless prominently use a particular musical idiom as the armature of their adaptations–Caleen Sinnette Jennings' *Hip-Hop Much Ado About Nothing* (2004) and *Mariachi Much Ado About Nothing* (2006, directed by Tony Plana for the East L.A. Classic Theater). Jennings, a noted adaptor of Shakespeare to African-American culture, transfers the action from the court to a contemporary hip-hop club; Benedick and Beatrice confess their love for one another not through sonnets but through cell phone texting. The *Mariachi Much Ado* prominently features Mexican music throughout, part of the production's reflection of the multiethnic heritage of Los Angeleno culture in costume, language, and setting. In this adaptation, Benedick and Claudio are Mexican soldiers who, upon their return home from war in 1862, fall in love with two Anglo women, Beatrice and Hero—a retelling that adds an element of ethnic tension to the lovers' courtships.

Of particular interest is *The Boys Are Coming Home* (2006, music and lyrics by Leslie Arden, book by Berni Stapledon). This ambitious, loose adaptation resituates the action of *Much Ado* in 1945, immediately after the Second World War, when the return of servicemen from combat and the shift from swing to bebop signaled profound changes in American life, particularly for working women who'd had a taste of liberation during the war. Bea, a riveter reminiscent of the famous icon Rosie the Riveter, and Ben, a free-thinking soldier, are feisty lovers tricked into love by their friends. They are juxtaposed with Charlie, a returning soldier, and Helen, his devoted girlfriend, whom Charlie mistakenly believes is having an affair with another man and whom he cruelly jilts at the altar. A subplot introduces a forbidden interracial romance between another couple, Maggie and Brad. Interestingly, although Helen's innocence is eventually established, she does not forgive Charlie as Hero does Claudio, but insists instead on the two first rebuilding trust. It is a mark of this adaptation's serious ambitions that it excises the low comedy of Dogberry and his men.

"HEY, NONNY, NONNY," "SIGH NO MORE," AND MUSICAL ADAPTATION

Though *Much Ado* does not feature a famous speech, the song "Sigh No More, Ladies," sung by Balthasar in Act 2, scene 3 as part of the men's prompting of Benedick to fall in love with Beatrice, has perennially attracted composers. Arthur Sullivan (of Gilbert and Sullivan fame) wrote a jaunty music-hall setting of the song as part of a set of five Shakespeare songs published in 1866. Of a more pastoral classical bent are the settings by the American composer Virgil Thomson and British composer Roger Quilter, both as part of their Shakespearean song cycles. Classical composers Peter Warlock, David Amram, and Kenneth Leighton also have crafted music for Shakespeare's lyrics. The song plays a prominent role in Kenneth Branagh's screen adaptation. The film begins with Beatrice's recitation of the lyrics over composer

Patrick Doyle's poignant musical setting, and ends with the entire cast singing the song in a triumphal choral performance. Doyle himself plays the role of Balthasar and performs the song, in character, during the garden scene.

Popular composers also have reset "Sigh No More" to a variety of musical styles. Country- and folk-inflected versions, for example, have been produced by Joe Hillyer (on his *Bard Americana* CD, 2003) and Ken Kleinfeld (on his *Shakespeare Songs* CD, 2005). The song becomes a delicate ballad when it appears in Ray Leslee's *Standup Shakespeare: A Cabaret Revue* (1995). Jazz settings are surprisingly abundant. A recording by Bob Crosby (brother of Bing) and his orchestra dating from 1939 offers a clever and very appealing swing arrangement, one of four novelty Shakespearean settings arranged by Arthur Young for Crosby's band, all sung by Marion Mann (reissued on the CD *Them There Eyes*). Pianist Dick Hyman teamed with vocalist Maxine Sullivan to offer a mid-tempo bop version on *Sullivan Shakespeare Hyman* (1971). "Sigh No More" becomes a sprightly calypso tune in Bess Bonnier's *Sweet William: A Jazz Cantata* (1999), and Martin Pickett's setting on his album *I'll Be With You Again* (2005) tends in the direction of funk. Though it is not a setting of Shakespeare's lyrics, Noel Coward's "Sigh No More" (from his 1945 revue of the same name) bears a certain family resemblance to Shakespeare's song, particularly in its melancholic exhortation to move on after being romantically betrayed; reportedly it was one of Coward's favorite tunes. Interestingly, a 1916 poem by D. H. Lawrence also bears the title "Sigh No More" and seems to evoke many of the themes of Shakespeare's song, despite the fact that Lawrence's poem concerns the narrator's discontent with birdsongs.)

"IT MAY BE I GO UNDER THAT TITLE": VARIATIONS ON A PHRASE

The play's title has become perhaps its most readily recognizable element for modern audiences. "Much ado about nothing" has become a favorite phrase on which popular culture has rung changes. Very few of these variations on the title have a direct or even indirect relationship to the plot or characters of Shakespeare's play. A list of examples gives a sense of the phrase's popularity:

- *Much Ado About Me* (comedian Fred Allen's memoir)
- "Much Ado About Mousing" (an episode of *Tom and Jerry*, an animated cartoon)
- *Much Ado About Calculus* (a mathematics textbook)
- *Much Ado About Prom Night* (a young adult novel)
- *Much Ado About Murder* (several mystery novels)
- *Much Ado About Aldo* (a children's book)
- *Mulch Ado About Nothing* (a mystery novel)
- "Much Ado About Nutting" (an animated cartoon about a squirrel struggling to crack open a coconut)
- *Much Ado About Loving* (a dramatic farce)
- "Much Ado About Knotting" and "Much Ado About Nagging" (episodes of *The Red Skelton Hour*, a variety show)
- *Much Ado About Dolls* (a manual on doll-collecting)
- "Much Ado About Dick" (an episode of the sitcom *3rd Rock from the Sun*)
- "Much Ado About Scrooge" (an episode of *Duck Tales*, the Disney animated series)
- "Much Ado" (an episode of the teen drama series *Party of Five*)

Though "much ado" is often used as a generic indicator of a farce or light-hearted treatment of a subject, several of these titles seem oblivious to Shakespeare's original meaning: a flurry of anxious activity about a nonconsequential matter. A few use the phrase to gesture toward some element of Shakespearean content: in Paula Cohen's novel *Much Ado About Jessie Kaplan* (2004), the title character, a widow, remembers that she was Shakespeare's "Dark Lady" in a previous life; Michael Rubbo's 2003 BBC documentary *Much Ado About Something* posits that Christopher Marlowe was not killed in a tavern duel but lived on to ghostwrite Shakespeare's plays. Only very occasionally do "much ado" titles indicate a connection, however oblique, with Shakespeare's play. Malia Martin's romance novel *Much Ado About Love* (2000) is just such a rare example. In it the protagonist, Sir Ian Terrance, discovers that the author of Shakespeare's works is in fact Olivia Tudor, bastard sister to Queen Elizabeth; his battle of wills and wits with Olivia (who calls herself "Beatrice") resembles that between Benedick and Beatrice.

THE AFTERLIVES OF BEATRICE, BENEDICK, AND DOGBERRY

Arguably, *Much Ado* has had the greatest impact upon popular culture not through adaptations of its story line or allusions to its dialogue, but rather through two enduring character types. Beatrice and Benedick, the lovers whose repartee masks the fact that they cannot admit their mutual attraction, stand at the head of a genealogy of couples whose bantering or bickering has an unmistakable erotic spark.

Spencer Tracy and Katherine Hepburn in Adam's Rib (1949).
© Underwood & Underwood/CORBIS

That genealogy stretches from Millamant and Mirabell in William Congreve's *The Way of the World* (1700) to Elizabeth and Darcy in Jane Austen's *Pride and Prejudice* (1813); couples in such screwball comedies as *It Happened One Night* (1934) and *The Awful Truth* (1937); William Powell and Myrna Loy in the *Thin Man* series; Spencer Tracy and Katherine Hepburn in *Adam's Rib* (1949); Han Solo and Princess Leia of the *Star Wars* films; and, most recently, such television series couples as David Addison and Maddie Hayes in *Moonlighting,* Sam Malone and Diane Chambers in *Cheers*, and Buffy and Spike in *Buffy the Vampire Slayer*. Such couples appear in all manner of popular genres, as exemplified, for example, by the recent film *Mr. and Mrs. Smith* (2005), which works the bickering-yet-loving-couple motif from *Much Ado* into the conventions of modern action films. This motif registers more obliquely in the conventions of romance novels where, in one much-used plotline, an initially contentious relationship between the heroine and a man evolves into erotic passion that is lent special piquancy by the tension between the lovers. Paula Marshall's *Dear Lady Disdain* (the title alludes to Benedick's snide name for Beatrice in Shakespeare's play), Georgette Heyer's *Friday's Child*, and Michelle Martin's *The Hampshire Hoyden* offer apt examples. Indeed, scholar Laurie Osborne–who has written extensively on Shakespeare and romance novels–suggests that *The Hampshire Hoyden* is a thoroughgoing reworking of *Much Ado About Nothing*, with the banter between the lovers based upon witty exchanges of Shakespeare quotations.

Equally enduring has been the type established by the verbally bumbling, vainglorious Dogberry the constable, one of several variations Shakespeare rang in his career on a venerable character from Latin comedy, the *miles gloriosus* or braggart soldier. Dogberry provided an important template not

Emma Thompson and Kenneth Branagh as Beatrice and Benedick in Branagh's film (1993).
© Sygma/Corbis

only for drama's most famous mangler of language, Mrs. Malaprop from Richard Brinsley Sheridan's *The Rivals* (1775), but also for such modern pop-culture characters as Alf Garnett, the malaproprism-prone protagonist of the British TV series *Till Death Do Us Part* (recast for American television as Archie Bunker on the influential TV show *All in the Family*). Dogberry's self-importance and comic earnestness as a officer of the law may also have been the model for Inspector Clouseau of the *Pink Panther* film series, and for Barney Fife, the much-beloved, comically inept deputy in the TV series *The Andy Griffith Show*. Whether these popular variations on Shakespeare's characters reveal the universality of his characterizations or simply pop culture's relentless recycling of audience-tested character types is a matter for some debate. In any case, the sheer number and range of variations on these characters testifies to the perennial popularity and wide-ranging influence of character types that Shakespeare memorably established in *Much Ado*.

Much Ado ABROAD

The language-based humor of *Much Ado* may have somewhat discouraged non-English adaptations of the play, for relatively few exist. On film the play has been modestly popular with Russian and Eastern European directors. Two major Soviet film versions have been produced, a relatively faithful rendition directed by L. Zamkovoy in 1956 (under the title *Mnogo shuma iz nichego*) and a rather loose adaptation directed by Tatyana Berezantseva in 1983 (under the title *Lyubovyu za lyubov* and featuring the music of Tikhon Khrennikov, who earlier had produced a comic operetta based on the play). Two other non-English film versions are curious relics from the Cold War. In 1958, West German director Ludwig Berger produced a modest TV version under the title *Viel Lärm um nichts*. Not to be outdone, six years later East Germany produced a lavish film version of its own under the direction of Martin Hellberg. Also entitled *Viel Lärm um nichts*, Hellberg's film, a period production of the play, was designed to showcase the technical capabilities of DEFA, the state East German film production company; though shot on a sound stage, Hellberg's production adapted Shakespeare's script with the film medium in mind and so may be counted as the first truly cinematic adaptation of *Much Ado*. Non-English adaptations in other media are rather more rare. *Enn ta Senn dan Vid* (1995) is a loose translation-adaptation by

Dev Virahsawmy, a Mauritian writer who has crafted many Shakespeare plays to an African idiom. And Japanese productions have experimented with free adaptations of the play–examples include the Takarazuka Revue Company's *Sweet Little Rock 'n' Roll* (1985, a contemporary musical version with all the parts played by women) and Noda Hideki's 1990 production (which grafted elements from *Othello* and *Romeo and Juliet* onto *Much Ado*).

More recently, Jiang Weiguo has converted Shakespeare's comedy to the conventions of *huangmeixi*, a operatic form indigenous to the Anhui province of China. This musical production–the title translates as *Looking for Trouble*–is of some historical significance, for it was premiered at China's first Shakespeare Festival in 1986, an event that signaled a decisive break with the destructive legacy of the Cultural Revolution. At the time controversial in China, *Looking for Trouble* was among the first productions to adapt Shakespeare to Chinese artistic idioms. Of special interest is how the production re-imagined the independent and aristocratic Beatrice (Bicui in this production) for a culture in which the only acceptable model of feminine assertiveness was the then-outmoded masculinized heroine of Soviet realism. In this adaptation, Bicui's feistiness accords with the dominance accorded the *dan*, or female role, in *huangmeixi* theater. *Looking for Trouble* is made psychologically plausible by the fact that the heroine grows up without parents in a rural border region under the tutelage of her uncle. Given the historical significance of this production, it is possible to see Bicui as a metaphor for China's new openness to Western culture and cultural assertiveness in the late 80s. (For a fuller description of *Looking for Trouble*, see Ruru Li, "Negotiating Intercultural Spaces," in *World-Wide Shakespeares*, ed. Sonia Massai, Routledge, 2005, pp. 40-44.)

BRANAGH'S *Much Ado About Nothing* (1993)

No discussion of popular adaptations of *Much Ado* can neglect Kenneth Branagh's 1993 film, a landmark among the many Shakespeare films produced in the 1990s. Following on the heels of his 1989 film adaptation of *Henry V*, *Much Ado* consolidated what would become the characteristics of Branagh's style for his Shakespeare films—in effect, updating Franco Zeffirelli's techniques for a more contemporary middlebrow audience:

- an all-star, often international cast;
- an emphasis upon narrative clarity;
- idiomatic, conversational (rather than declamatory) delivery of the lines;
- interludes of lush visual spectacle;
- liberal use of steadi-cam shooting to preserve the integrity of the actors' performances;
- an ensemble feeling to the production;
- musical score underlining the emotional content of scenes;
- an extended, unbroken bravura shot that includes all the film's cast (in this case, that shot ends the film).

Even though the film is set in nineteenth-century Italy, Branagh makes numerous allusions to contemporary popular culture. The Tuscan landscape is photographed like a travel poster or postcard, and there is a wry acknowledgement in the film's witty opening shot; the heroic return of Don Pedro's men from battle not only subtly links the action back to the victorious military campaign in Branagh's previous Shakespeare film, but it also evokes the signature shot of men on horseback from *The Magnificent Seven*. Michael Keaton's eccentric rendition of Dogberry recalls the pantomime-horse gag from *Monty Python and the Holy Grail*, and the chemistry between Branagh's Benedick and Emma Thompson's Beatrice was enlivened by then-current tabloid gossip about the celebrity couple. Branagh's approach was calculated to counter the reputation of Shakespearean film as highbrow art-house fare and to make Shakespeare palatable for cineplex audiences. At the time, it was one of the most financially successful Shakespeare films ever made, and it remains arguably Branagh's most successful Shakespearean film adaptation to date. More importantly, it exerted influence direct and indirect over many of the Shakespeare films that followed it in the 1990s.

Dramatis Personae

Don Pedro, Prince of Aragon
Claudio, a favorite of Don Pedro
Benedick, a favorite of Don Pedro
Balthasar, servant of Don Pedro

Don John, his bastard brother
Borachio, servant to Don John
Conrad, servant to Don John

Leonato, Governor of Messina
Hero, his daughter
Anthonio, his brother
Beatrice, niece to Leonato
Margaret, gentlewoman attending on Hero
Ursula, gentlewoman attending on Hero

Dogberry, a foolish officer
Verges, his second

Sexton, Friar, Boy, Messengers, Watch, and Attendants

[Much Ado About Nothing

Nothing

Act 1

0: Scene: The setting for Charles Kean's 1858 production at the Princess's Theatre: a sunset view of the Port of Messina, the sun gradually disappearing in the west, casting its declining rays on the houses and the ships, to be followed by the rising moon. Then a brilliant masquerade scene with variegated lights from garden and bridge lamps.

0: Stage Direction: ***INNOGEN***: Though the character has no lines and is sometimes cut from modernized texts, her visual presence may have had some significance and she is thus left in.

Kirsten Parker as Hero, Harriet Walter as Beatrice, Norma Dumezweni as Ursula, Christine Barreiro as Innogen, and Sarah Ball as Margaret in the RSC's 2002 production directed by Gregory Doran
Photo: Donald Cooper

1, 8: **Pedro:** the first two times the character is mentioned, the quarto and folio print "Peter"; editions since Nicholas Rowe (1709) have printed "Pedro"

1: **Aragon:** a region in northeastern Spain

2: **Messina:** a city on the island of Sicily, Italy

3: **three leagues:** about nine miles or fifteen kilometers (a league was intended to represent the distance a person could walk in an hour, about three miles or five kilometers)

6: **sort:** rank or importance

Act 1, Scene 1]

Enter LEONATO *Governor of Messina,* INNOGEN *his wife,*
HERO *his daughter, and* BEATRICE *his niece,*
with a MESSENGER

LEONATO
I learn in this letter that Don Pedro of Aragon comes this night to
Messina.

MESSENGER
He is very near by this. He was not three leagues off when I left
him.

LEONATO
How many gentlemen have you lost in this action? 5

MESSENGER
But few of any sort and none of name.

LEONATO
A victory is twice itself when the achiever brings home full
numbers. I find here that Don Pedro hath bestowed much honor
on a young Florentine called Claudio.

MESSENGER
Much deserved on his part, and, equally remembered by Don 10
Pedro, he hath borne himself beyond the promise of his age, doing,
in the figure of a lamb, the feats of a lion. He hath indeed better
bettered expectation than you must expect of me to tell you how.

LEONATO
He hath an uncle here in Messina, will be very much glad of it.

16–17: joy could not...badge of bitterness: Modesty dictates that he hide his joyful emotions, but they break forth in tears.

19: measure: abundance

20: truer: more sincere

23: Mountanto: suggesting both a fencing term (*montanto*, mentioned in Ben Jonson's comedy *Everyman in His Humour*) and perhaps Benedick's mountainous ego

23: "I pray you, is Signor Mountanto returned from the wars, or no?": Karen Ziemba as Beatrice and the cast of the Shakespeare Theatre Company's 2002-2003 production directed by Mark Lamos
Photo: Carol Rosegg

29: set up his bills...challenged Cupid at the flight: Beatrice suggests that Benedick is both a tradesman and a quarreler.

31: burbolt: an arrow fired from a crossbow, sometimes modernized as "bird-bolt." Benedick claims to be a better archer than Cupid, who fires arrows of love.

32: killed and eaten: As in *Henry V*: "*Ramburer*. He longs to eat the English. / *Constable*. I think he will eat all he kills" (3.8).

MESSENGER

I have already delivered him letters, and there appears much joy   15
in him, even so much that joy could not show itself modest
enough without a badge of bitterness.

LEONATO

Did he break out into tears?

MESSENGER

In great measure.

LEONATO

A kind overflow of kindness; there are no faces truer then those   20
that are so washed. How much better is it to weep at joy than to
joy at weeping!

BEATRICE

I pray you, is Signor Mountanto returned from the wars, or no?

MESSENGER

I know none of that name, lady. There was none such in the army
of any sort.   25

LEONATO

What is he that you ask for niece?

HERO

My cousin means Signor Benedick of Padua.

MESSENGER

O, he's returned, and as pleasant as ever he was.

BEATRICE

He set up his bills here in Messina and challenged Cupid at the
flight, and my uncle's fool, reading the challenge, subscribed for   30
Cupid, and challenged him at the burbolt. I pray you, how many
hath he killed and eaten in these wars? But how many hath he
killed? For indeed, I promised to eat all of his killing.

37: **musty victual:** stale food, playing on the sense of eating all he kills; **holp:** helped, though in the theatre it may sound like "hope"

38: **trencher-man:** one who has a hearty appetite

43: **stuffed man:** suggesting that he is full of himself or egotistical

48-50: "In our last conflict, four of his five wits went halting off, and now is the whole man governed with one": Kristen Johnston as Beatrice, Elizabeth Waterston as Hero, and Sam Waterston as Leonato in The Public Theater 2004 production directed by David Esbjornson
Photo: Michal Daniel

50: **warm:** His *sparking* wit *fires* with creativity. She then suggests he's as witty as a horse.

53-54: **sworn brother:** brother-in arms, perhaps echoing *Henry V*: "For he today that sheds his blood with me/ Shall be my brother." (4.3)

LEONATO

'Faith niece, you tax Signor Benedick too much, but he'll be meet
with you, I doubt it not.   35

MESSENGER

He hath done good service, lady, in these wars.

BEATRICE

You had musty victual, and he hath holp to eat it. He is a very
valiant trencher-man; he hath an excellent stomach.

MESSENGER

And a good soldier too, lady.

BEATRICE

And a good soldier to a lady. But what is he to a lord?   40

MESSENGER

A lord to a lord, a man to a man, stuffed with all honorable
virtues.

BEATRICE

It is so indeed, he is no less then a stuffed man. But for the
stuffing—well, we are all mortal.

LEONATO

You must not, sir, mistake my niece. There is a kind of merry war   45
betwixt Signor Benedick and her. They never meet, but there's a
skirmish of wit between them.

BEATRICE

Alas, he gets nothing by that. In our last conflict, four of his five
wits went halting off, and now is the whole man governed with
one; so that if he have wit enough to keep himself warm, let him   50
bear it for a difference between himself and his horse, for it is all
the wealth that he hath left to be known a reasonable creature.
Who is his companion now? He hath every month a new-sworn
brother.

57: **next block:** newest fashion (a block was a mold used in the construction of hats). Shakespeare's brother, Gilbert, was a haberdasher.

58: **your books:** your favor

59: **an:** if

60: **squarer:** quarreler; from *Titus Andronicus*: "... are you such fools/ To square for this?" (2.1)

64: **presently:** immediately

65: **the Benedick:** suggestive of a disease; see 3.4.51.

71: Stage Direction: ***BASTARD:*** In Shakespeare, bastards often suggest both dubious parentage and a dark temperament.

MESSENGER
    Is't possible?   55

BEATRICE
    Very easily possible. He wears his faith but as the fashion of his
    hat; it ever changes with the next block.

MESSENGER
    I see, lady, the gentleman is not in your books.

BEATRICE
    No, an he were, I would burn my study. But I pray you, who is his
    companion? Is there no young squarer now that will make a   60
    voyage with him to the devil?

MESSENGER
    He is most in the company of the right noble Claudio.

BEATRICE
    O Lord, he will hang upon him like a disease. He is sooner caught
    than the pestilence, and the taker runs presently mad. God help
    the noble Claudio if he have caught the Benedick, it will cost him   65
    a thousand pound ere a be cured.

MESSENGER
    I will hold friends with you lady.

BEATRICE
    Do, good friend.

LEONATO
    You will never run mad, niece.

BEATRICE
    No, not till a hot January.   70

MESSENGER
    Don Pedro is approached.
                Enter DON PEDRO, CLAUDIO, BENEDICK, BALTHASAR,
                                    and JOHN THE BASTARD

77: **charge:** orders

79: **Were you in doubt:** playfully suggesting that Innogen has been false to Pedro's bed

81: **full:** perfectly

82: **Truly the lady fathers herself:** There is no mistaking who her father is (because of her resemblance to him).

84-85: **his head on her shoulders:** Benedick lightheartedly suggests that Hero's face is far more beautiful than her father's.

84-107: Scene: **If Signor Leonato be her father...I know you of old:** This first skirmish of words is set as an aside in the BBC TV version (1984); Kenneth Branagh (1993) stages it is a public demonstration of mutual hostility.

tracks 2-4

86-107:
Pauline Jameson as Beatrice and Richard Johnson as Benedick
Saskia Reeves as Beatrice and Samuel West as Benedick

87-90: **Lady Disdain...Courtesy:** Claire McEachern (2006) suggests that Benedick is referring to an allegorical figure, hence the capitalization.

DEAR·LADY
DISDAIN

88: "What, my dear Lady Disdain!": Engraving by Byam Shaw, from 1900
By permission of the Folger Shakespeare Library

89: **meet:** suitable

DON PEDRO
Good Signor Leonato, are you come to meet your trouble? The fashion of the world is to avoid cost, and you encounter it.

LEONATO
Never came trouble to my house in the likeness of your Grace, for trouble being gone, comfort should remain. But when you depart   75
from me, sorrow abides and happiness takes his leave.

DON PEDRO
You embrace your charge too willingly. I think this is your daughter.

LEONATO
Her mother hath many times told me so.

BENEDICK
Were you in doubt, sir, that you asked her?

LEONATO
Signor Benedick, no, for then were you a child.   80

DON PEDRO
You have it full, Benedick.We may guess by this what you are, being a man. Truly the lady fathers herself. Be happy lady, for you are like an honorable father.

BENEDICK
If Signor Leonato be her father, she would not have his head on her shoulders for all Messina, as like him as she is.   85

BEATRICE
I wonder that you will still be talking, Signor Benedick. Nobody marks you.

BENEDICK
What, my dear Lady Disdain! Are you yet living?

BEATRICE
Is it possible Disdain should die while she hath such meet food to feed it as Signor Benedick? Courtesy itself must convert to   90
Disdain, if you come in her presence.

tracks 2-4

86-107:
Pauline Jameson as Beatrice and Richard Johnson as Benedick
Saskia Reeves as Beatrice and Samuel West as Benedick

92: **turncoat:** one who forsakes his party or principles
96: **cold blood:** cold because it is not hot with passion

97-98: "I had rather hear my dog bark at a crow than a man swear he loves me.":
Dan Snook as Benedick and Karen Ziemba as Beatrice in the Shakespeare Theatre
Company's 2002-2003 production directed by Mark Lamos
Photo: Carol Rosegg

100: **predestinate:** inevitable
103: **parrot-teacher:** Beatrice repeats herself like a parrot.
106: **continuer:** one who carries on without tiring
107: **You always end with a jade's trick:** i.e., Benedick always finds some way to
back out of a bargain; Sheldon Zitner (1993) suggests a horse (jade) who refuses to
go forward.
108: **This is the sum of all, Leonato:** The folio prints: "This is the summe of all:
Leonato, signior *Claudio,* and signior *Benedicke,*" etc. However, in this construction
Don Pedro addresses Leonato to tell him that Leonato has requested that they all
stay at his house, which makes little sense. With a slight change to the punctuation,
Leonato is now told to listen as he informs Claudio and Benedick of Leonato's intent.

BENEDICK

Then is Courtesy a turncoat, but it is certain I am loved of all
ladies, only you excepted, and I would I could find in my heart
that I had not a hard heart, for truly I love none.

BEATRICE

A dear happiness to women. They would else have been troubled   95
with a pernicious suitor. I thank God and my cold blood I am of
your humor for that. I had rather hear my dog bark at a crow
than a man swear he loves me.

BENEDICK

God keep your ladyship still in that mind, so some gentleman or
other shall 'scape a predestinate scratched face.   100

BEATRICE

Scratching could not make it worse and 'twere such a face as
yours were.

BENEDICK

Well, you are a rare parrot-teacher.

BEATRICE

A bird of my tongue is better than a beast of yours.

BENEDICK

I would my horse had the speed of your tongue, and so good a   105
continuer. But keep your way. A God's name, I have done.

BEATRICE

You always end with a jade's trick. I know you of old.

DON PEDRO

This is the sum of all, Leonato, Signor Claudio, and Signor
Benedick; my dear friend Leonato hath invited you all. I tell him
we shall stay here at the least a month, and he heartily prays some   110
occasion may detain us longer. I dare swear he is no hypocrite but
prays from his heart.

119-213: Scene: **Benedick, didst thou note the daughter...and so I leave you:** The nineteenth-century actor William Macready displayed great humor in the role: he saw Benedick as "a sort of matrimonial theorist—ludicrous from the gravity with which he supports a favorite hypothesis, and not a crotchety individual with a curious temper needing mending."

tracks 5-7

119-150:
John Horton as Benedick and Bruce Armstrong as Claudio
Samuel West as Benedick and Jason O'Mara as Claudio

121: **modest:** proper

122: **simple:** honest

126: **low:** short; possibly also a reference to her lack of royal blood, as in "lowly"

126: **high praise:** great praise

129-130: "but as she is, I do not like her.": Eric Lander as Claudio and John Gielgud as Benedick in the 1950 RSC production directed by John Gielgud

Photo: Angus McBean © Royal Shakespeare Company

LEONATO

If you swear, my lord, you shall not be forsworn. *[To DON JOHN]* Let me bid you welcome, my lord, being reconciled to the Prince, your brother. I owe you all duty.   115

JOHN

I thank you. I am not of many words, but I thank you.

LEONATO

Please it your Grace lead on?

DON PEDRO

Your hand, Leonato. We will go together.
                    Exeunt all but BENEDICK and CLAUDIO

CLAUDIO

Benedick, didst thou note the daughter of Signor Leonato?

BENEDICK

I noted her not, but I looked on her.   120

CLAUDIO

Is she not a modest young lady?

BENEDICK

Do you question me as an honest man should do, for my simple true judgment, or would you have me speak after my custom, as being a professed tyrant to their sex?

CLAUDIO

No, I pray thee, speak in sober judgment.   125

BENEDICK

Why i'faith methinks she's too low for a high praise, too brown for a fair praise, and too little for a great praise. Only this commendation I can afford her, that were she other than she is, she were unhandsome, and being no other but as she is, I do not like her.   130

tracks 5-7

119-150:
John Horton as Benedick and Bruce Armstrong as Claudio
Samuel West as Benedick and Jason O'Mara as Claudio

131: **in sport:** joking

136: **flouting Jack:** a contemptuous troublemaker

136-7: **Or do you play...rare carpenter:** Benedick suggests that Claudio is not being serious. Saying he loves Hero is as silly as saying that Cupid uses his love darts to hunt rabbits or that Vulcan, who forged Achilles' armor, is a carpenter.

141: **cousin:** might refer to a close friend, hence the word *consanguineous*, as much as a family connection of some sort; **fury:** temper, possibly justified temper, as in the mythological Furies who punished wrongdoers. If so, Benedick admits that he has in the past "played false" with Beatrice's affections.

149: **yoke:** a wooden frame or collar fitted around the neck of an ox (or similar animal) for drawing a plow or vehicle; a symbol of servitude or slavery; **sigh away Sundays:** Claudio will spend even the day of rest, Sundays, dreaming of her.

150: Stage Direction: ***Enter DON PEDRO:*** The quarto and folio have Don John entering here, but he has no lines and seems unaware of Claudio's interest in Hero when he reenters in 1.3.0. Editors since Edward Capell (1768) have cut his entry here. In the BBC version (1984), Jon Finch's gay Don Pedro lisped, and held his hand dandily as he heard with great melancholy that Claudio (Robert Reynolds) was in love with a woman.

CLAUDIO

Thou thinkest I am in sport. I pray thee tell me truly how thou
likest her.

BENEDICK

Would you buy her, that you enquire after her?

CLAUDIO

Can the world buy such a jewel?

BENEDICK

Yea, and a case to put it into, but speak you this with a sad brow?   135
Or do you play the flouting Jack to tell us Cupid is a good hare-
finder and Vulcan a rare carpenter? Come, in what key shall a
man take you to go in the song?

CLAUDIO

In mine eye, she is the sweetest lady that ever I looked on.

BENEDICK

I can see yet without spectacles, and I see no such matter. There's   140
her cousin, an she were not possessed with a fury, exceeds her as
much in beauty, as the first of May doth the last of December–But
I hope you have no intent to turn husband, have you?

CLAUDIO

I would scarce trust myself, though I had sworn the contrary, if
Hero would be my wife.   145

BENEDICK

Is't come to this? In faith, hath not the world one man but he will
wear his cap with suspicion? Shall I never see a bachelor of three
score again? Go to, i'faith, an thou wilt needs thrust thy neck into
a yoke, wear the print of it and sigh away Sundays–Look, Don
Pedro is returned to seek you.   150

Enter DON PEDRO

DON PEDRO

What secret hath held you here that you followed not to Leonato's?

155-156: "But on my allegiance, mark you this, on my allegiance! He is in love.": John Gielgud as Benedick, Eric Lander as Claudio, and Leon Quartermaine as Don Pedro in the 1950 RSC production directed by John Gielgud

Photo: Angus McBean © Royal Shakespeare Company

160: **Like the old tale:** i.e., like a tale of romance

164: **fetch me in:** make fun of me

167: **by my two faiths and troths:** In swearing by both faiths (his allegiance to Don Pedro and to Claudio), Benedick is in fact being unfaithful.

BENEDICK
I would your Grace would constrain me to tell.

DON PEDRO
I charge thee on thy allegiance.

BENEDICK
You hear, Count Claudio, I can be secret as a dumb man; I would
have you think so. But on my allegiance, mark you this, on my   155
allegiance! He is in love. With who? Now that is your Grace's
part. Mark how short his answer is: with Hero, Leonato's short
daughter.

CLAUDIO
If this were so, so were it uttered.

BENEDICK
Like the old tale, my lord, it is not so, nor 'twas not so. But,   160
indeed, God forbid, it should be so.

CLAUDIO
If my passion change not shortly, God forbid it should be otherwise.

DON PEDRO
Amen, if you love her, for the lady is very well worthy.

CLAUDIO
You speak this to fetch me in, my lord.

DON PEDRO
By my troth, I speak my thought.   165

CLAUDIO
And in faith, my lord, I spoke mine.

BENEDICK
And by my two faiths and troths, my lord, I spoke mine.

CLAUDIO
That I love her, I feel.

173: **in the despite:** for rejecting or disdaining

174: **force of his will:** William Warburton (1747) suggests that Claudio is replying to Benedick's heretic metaphor—"heresy" being here defined as flouting the will of Scripture.

177: **rechate:** a whistle used to train hunting dogs, often modernized as *recheat*. Actaeon, a symbol of uncontrolled sexual passion, was torn to pieces by hunting dogs; Benedick suggests that he would be similarly victimized if he were domesticated by women.

177-178: **hang my bugle in an invisible baldric:** a "baldric" is a sheath for a sword. The inference here is that Benedick fears to put his instrument (sword/horn/penis) in a woman's sheath (baldric/case/vagina).

185: **ballad-maker:** a composer of both erotic and love songs

186-187: **blind Cupid:** Benedick suggests that the symbol of love is better suited to whorehouses than the marriage bed.

190: **hang me...shoot at me:** possibly in reference to the cruel sport of firing arrows at cats in wooden baskets

191: **Adam:** Lewis Theobald (1733) reads this as a reference to Adam Bell, a famous archer, but Benedick may well be thinking of the biblical Adam, who was fooled by Eve.

DON PEDRO

That she is worthy, I know.

BENEDICK

That I neither feel how she should be loved, nor know how she   170
should be worthy is the opinion that fire cannot melt out of me. I
will die in it at the stake.

DON PEDRO

Thou wast ever an obstinate heretic in the despite of beauty.

CLAUDIO

And never could maintain his part but in the force of his will.

BENEDICK

That a woman conceived me, I thank her; that she brought me   175
up, I likewise give her most humble thanks. But that I will have
a rechate winded in my forehead, or hang my bugle in an invisible baldric, all women shall pardon me. Because I will not do
them the wrong to mistrust any, I will do myself the right to trust
none. And the fine is, for the which I may go the finer, I will live   180
a bachelor.

DON PEDRO

I shall see thee ere I die look pale with love.

BENEDICK

With anger, with sickness, or with hunger, my lord, not with love.
Prove that ever I lose more blood with love than I will get again
with drinking, pick out mine eyes with a ballad-maker's pen and   185
hang me up at the door of a brothel house for the sign of blind
Cupid.

DON PEDRO

Well, if ever thou dost fall from this faith, thou wilt prove a
notable argument.

BENEDICK

If I do, hang me in a bottle like a cat and shoot at me, and he that   190
hits me, let him be clapped on the shoulder and called Adam.

192: time shall try: time will tell

192: In time...the yoke: (proverbial) Even the wild bull is eventually domesticated.

93-94: "The savage bull may, but if ever the sensible Benedick bear it, pluck off the bull's horns and set them on my forehead": Sherman Howard as Benedick in The Shakespeare Theatre of New Jersey's 2003 production directed by Bonnie J. Monte
Photo: Gerry Goodstein

198: horn mad: raving mad, possibly as a result of a woman's infidelity ("horn" is a reference to the horns of a cuckold, a man whose wife has been unfaithful)

199-201: quiver...quake...earthquake: Cupid's arrows are kept in a quiver. Quivering and quake may suggest how shaken one is by love, hence Benedick's suggestion that if he falls in love, that the world will quake with the sudden and unexpected change.

202: you will temporize the hours: Don Pedro may mean, "Well, you're good fun to pass time with," or "You will come to see the truth of what I say in time."

203: repair: go

206: embassage: message conveyed by an ambassador

208-209: "To the tuition of God...loving friend, Benedick": Claudio and Pedro banter with formal addresses such as Benedick might use in an embassage.

209: sixth of July: Midsummer Day, a traditional date for midsummer madness. Claire McEachern (2006) suggests that this was the day quarterly rents were due and, thus, a likely day to write letters.

DON PEDRO
Well, as time shall try. In time the savage bull doth bear the yoke.

BENEDICK
The savage bull may, but if ever the sensible Benedick bear it, pluck off the bull's horns and set them in my forehead, and let me be vilely painted and in such great letters as they write, "Here is   195 good horse to hire." Let them signify under my sign: "Here you may see Benedick, the married man."

CLAUDIO
If this should ever happen, thou wouldst be horn mad.

DON PEDRO
Nay, if Cupid have not spent all his quiver in Venice, thou wilt quake for this shortly.   200

BENEDICK
I look for an earthquake too then.

DON PEDRO
Well, you will temporize with the hours. In the meantime, good Signor Benedick, repair to Leonato's. Commend me to him and tell him I will not fail him at supper, for indeed he hath made great preparation.   205

BENEDICK
I have almost matter enough in me for such an embassage, and so I commit you.

CLAUDIO
"To the tuition of God. From my house," if I had it.

DON PEDRO
"The sixth of July. Your loving friend, Benedick."

210: **body of your discourse:** i.e., construction of your argument (the metaphor of this passage is from tailoring)

211: **guarded:** trimmed, adorned; **guards:** ornaments or decorations; **slightly basted:** lightly or loosely sewn

212: **old ends:** old sayings i.e., that even bulls are eventually domesticated. Benedick suggests that Claudio examine his own situation before making fun of him.

215: **to teach:** to do some good

218: **Hath Leonato any son:** Claudio is inquiring as to whether he might inherit Leonato's entire estate.

220: **affect:** love

231: **book of words:** a proper, perhaps even memorized, speech declaring love

BENEDICK

    Nay mock not, mock not. The body of your discourse is sometime   210
    guarded with fragments, and the guards are but slightly basted on
    neither. Ere you flout old ends any further, examine your
    conscience, and so I leave you.

                                                              Exit

CLAUDIO

    My liege, your highness now may do me good.

DON PEDRO

    My love is thine to teach. Teach it but how,   215
    And thou shalt see how apt it is to learn
    Any hard lesson that may do thee good.

CLAUDIO

    Hath Leonato any son, my lord?

DON PEDRO

    No child but Hero; she's his only heir.
    Dost thou affect her Claudio?

CLAUDIO

                  O my lord,   220
    When you went onward on this ended action,
    I looked upon her with a soldier's eye,
    That liked but had a rougher task in hand
    Than to drive liking to the name of love.
    But now I am returned, and that war-thoughts   225
    Have left their places vacant in their rooms,
    Come thronging soft and delicate desires,
    All prompting me how fair young Hero is.
    Saying I liked her ere I went to wars–

DON PEDRO

    Thou wilt be like a lover presently   230
    And tire the hearer with a book of words.
    If thou dost love fair Hero, cherish it,
    And I will break with her and with her father,
    And thou shalt have her. Was't not to this end
    That thou began'st to twist so fine a story?   235

237: **his complexion:** appearance. Claudio is saying he looks sick with love.

239: **salved:** smoothed over; **treatise:** story or explanation

240: **What need...than the flood:** i.e., why say more than is needed

242-243: **Thou lovest...remedy:** i.e., as Claudio is sick with love, Don Pedro will offer a cure

244: **reveling:** a party

247: **unclasp:** The folio has "unclaipe," a typographical error; the quarto has "unclaspe."

248: **take her hearing prisoner:** overpower her with my words

250: **to her father I will break:** I will work out the marriage dowry with her father.

CLAUDIO

How sweetly you do minister to love
That know love's grief by his complexion!
But lest my liking might too sudden seem,
I would have salved it with a longer treatise.

DON PEDRO

What need the bridge much broader than the flood?   240
The fairest grant is the necessity.
Look what will serve is fit. 'Tis once. Thou lovest,
And I will fit thee with the remedy.
I know we shall have reveling tonight,
I will assume thy part in some disguise   245
And tell fair Hero I am Claudio,
And in her bosom I'll unclasp my heart
And take her hearing prisoner with the force
And strong encounter of my amorous tale.
Then after, to her father will I break,   250
And the conclusion is, she shall be thine.
In practice let us put it presently.

Exeunt

6: **As the events stamps them:** as the events unfold

7-8: **thick-pleached alley:** a thick hedge of intertwining branches; thus, a place where Benedick can hide unobserved

9: **discovered:** revealed

11: **accordant:** willing

11-12: **take the present time by the top:** perhaps akin to our expression, "take the bull by the horns"

17: **peradventure:** perhaps

18: **Cousin:** The quarto and folio have "coosins" ("cousins"), but only one person is on stage with Leonato. Claire McEachern (2006) has Anthonio exit and a variety of attendants enter and cross the stage. Why servants would be called cousins and soon after "friend" is not explained. The problem remains if Leonato is referring only to his brother. Why call his brother "friend," a term which suggests only a passing acquaintance? In terms of a solution, the main issue is whether we should, as McEachern does, add characters and stage business to account for the pluralization of "cousins" or merely trim the plural to singular. The latter is far less intrusive than adding an early exit for Anthonio and then the entry of a variety of characters who serve no other purpose except to be immediately dismissed by Leonato.

20: **skill:** the quarto prints "shill," an evident error

Gary Waldhorn as Leonato in the 2002 RSC production directed by Gregory Doran
Photo: J. Dockar-Drysdale © Royal Shakespeare Company

Enter LEONATO and an OLD MAN [ANTHONIO], brother to LEONATO

LEONATO

How now, brother, where is my cousin, your son? Hath he
provided this music?

ANTHONIO

He is very busy about it, but brother, I can tell you strange news
that you yet dreamt not of.

LEONATO

Are they good?   5

ANTHONIO

As the events stamps them, but they have a good cover; they show
well outward. The Prince and Count Claudio, walking in a thick-
pleached alley in mine orchard, were thus much overheard by a
man of mine. The Prince discovered to Claudio that he loved my
niece, your daughter, and meant to acknowledge it this night in a   10
dance, and if he found her accordant, he meant to take the present time by the top and instantly break with you of it.

LEONATO

Hath the fellow any wit that told you this?

ANTHONIO

A good sharp fellow, I will send for him and question him yourself.

LEONATO

No, no; we will hold it as a dream till it appear itself. But I will   15
acquaint my daughter withal, that she may be the better prepared
for an answer, if peradventure this be true. Go you and tell her of
it. Cousin, you know what you have to do.
                                          [Momentarily lost in his thoughts]
O I cry you mercy, friend, go you with me and I will use your skill.
Good cousin, have a care this busy time.   20
                                                                                     Exeunt

tracks 8-10

1-47:
Don Meyers as Conrad, David Renton as Don John, and Edwin Rubin as Borachio
Alex Lowe as Conrad, Steve Hodson as Don John, and Eddie Marsan as Borachio

0: Scene: In the BBC version (1984), Don John (Vernon Dobtcheff) was gray-bearded and bald; in Branagh's film (1993), a twenty-something Keanu Reeves (in black leather) played Don John.

1: **What the good year:** perhaps no more than "How you doing" though Sheldon Zitner (1993) suggests "What the hell"; **out of measure:** beyond limits i.e., exceedingly

6: **sufferance:** endurance

8: **Saturn:** a planet thought to have melancholy influence; **moral medicine:** medicine of philosophy or moral precepts

8-9: **mortifying mischief:** deadly disease

12: **claw:** flatter or fawn over

15: **controlment:** restraint

16: **ta'en:** taken

19-20: **It is needful...own harvest:** Conrad suggests that if Don John expects to prosper, i.e., reap the rewards of a good harvest, he should be nice to his brother. See *Macbeth*: "Duncan. I have begun to plant thee, and will labour / To make thee full of growing. / *Banquo.* There if I grow/ The harvest is your own" (1.4).

Act 1, Scene 3]

Enter JOHN THE BASTARD and CONRAD his companion

CONRAD
What the good year, my lord, why are you thus out of measure sad?

JOHN
There is no measure in the occasion that breeds; therefore the sad-
ness is without limit.

CONRAD
You should hear reason.

JOHN
And when I have heard it, what blessing brings it?   5

CONRAD
If not a present remedy, at least a patient sufferance.

JOHN
I wonder that thou, being, as thou say'st thou art, born under
Saturn, goest about to apply a moral medicine to a mortifying
mischief? I cannot hide what I am. I must be sad when I have
cause and smile at no man's jests; eat when I have stomach and   10
wait for no man's leisure; sleep when I am drowsy and tend on no
man's business; laugh when I am merry and claw no man in his
humor.

CONRAD
Yea, but you must not make the full show of this till you may do
it without controlment. You have of late stood out against your   15
brother, and he hath ta'en you newly into his grace, where it is
impossible you should take true root but by the fair weather that
you make yourself. It is needful that you frame the season for your
own harvest.

tracks 8-10

1-47:
Don Meyers as Conrad, David Renton as Don John, and Edwin Rubin as Borachio
Alex Lowe as Conrad, Steve Hodson as Don John, and Eddie Marsan as Borachio

20-22: "I had rather be a canker in a hedge than a rose in his grace, and it better fits my blood to be disdained of all than to fashion a carriage to rob love from any.": David Hyde Pierce as Don John in the New York Public Theater's 1987 production directed by Gerald Freedman

Photo: George E. Joseph

20: **canker in a hedge than a rose in his grace:** a thorn in his side than a source of pleasure to him

21-22: **fashion a carriage:** disguise who I really am

24: **enfranchised:** freed

25: **clog:** a chain or weight that keeps him in place

29: Stage Direction: ***Enter BORACHIO:*** The quarto and folio have him enter a line later; this is the emendation of Edward Capell (1768).

32: **intelligence:** news

37: **exquisite:** said ironically. John blames Claudio for his recent defeat.

39: **proper:** again, meant ironically

JOHN

I had rather be a canker in a hedge than a rose in his grace, and 20
it better fits my blood to be disdained of all than to fashion a
carriage to rob love from any. In this, though I cannot be said to
be a flattering honest man, it must not be denied but I am a plain-
dealing villain. I am trusted with a muzzle and enfranchised with
a clog, therefore I have decreed not to sing in my cage. If I had my 25
mouth, I would bite; if I had my liberty, I would do my liking. In
the meantime, let me be that I am, and seek not to alter me.

CONRAD

Can you make no use of your discontent?

JOHN

I make all use of it, for I use it only. Who comes here?

Enter BORACHIO

What news Borachio? 30

BORACHIO

I came yonder from a great supper. The Prince, your brother, is
royally entertained by Leonato, and I can give you intelligence of
an intended marriage.

JOHN

Will it serve for any model to build mischief on? What is he for a
fool that betroths himself to unquietness? 35

BORACHIO

Marry, it is your brother's right hand.

JOHN

Who, the most exquisite Claudio?

BORACHIO

Even he.

JOHN

A proper squire, and who, and who, which way looks he?

1-47:
Don Meyers as Conrad, David Renton as Don John, and Edwin Rubin as Borachio
Alex Lowe as Conrad, Steve Hodson as Don John, and Eddie Marsan as Borachio

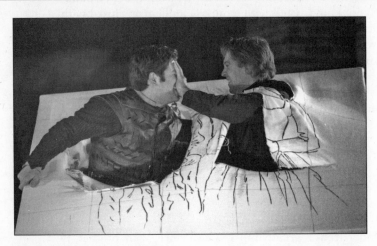

Patrick Baladi as Borachio and Damien Lewis as Don John in the 1996 RSC production directed by Michael Boyd

Photo: Reg Wilson © Royal Shakespeare Company

41: march-chick: often printed as "March chick" or, following the folio and quarto, "March-chick," both suggestive of a spring hatchling. John suggests that Hero (the chick) is overeager to jump (quick to march) into bed with Claudio. The line was cut in Branagh's film (1993) for fear that Keanu Reeves' American enunciation of "chick" would be understood as reverting to "Bill-and-Ted" surfer slang.

42: perfumer: someone who perfumed rooms, perhaps a housemaid

44: arras: curtains or tapestry hangings, where, famously, Polonius hid in his observation of Hamlet

48: start-up: a newcomer, sometime associated with Shakespeare himself; Robert Greene referred to Shakespeare as an "upstart crow" (see *In the Age of Shakespeare*)

48-49: If I can cross...bless myself every way: Playing on religious terminology, John suggests that each time he crosses or thwarts Claudio he betters or blesses himself.

49: sure: dependable

53: Would the cook...mind: The implication is that he would like to poison everyone; **of:** the quarto prints "a"

BORACHIO

Marry, on Hero, the daughter and heir of Leonato.   40

JOHN

A very forward march-chick, how came you to this?

BORACHIO

Being entertained for a perfumer, as I was smoking a musty room,
comes me the Prince and Claudio hand in hand in sad conference.
I whipped me behind the arras, and there heard it agreed upon
that the Prince should woo Hero for himself and, having obtained   45
her, give her to Count Claudio.

JOHN

Come, come, let us thither; this may prove food to my displeasure.
That young start-up hath all the glory of my overthrow. If I can
cross him any way, I bless myself every way. You are both sure,
and will assist me?   50

CONRAD

To the death, my lord.

JOHN

Let us to the great supper. Their cheer is the greater that I am
subdued. Would the cook were of my mind. Shall we go prove
what's to be done?

BORACHIO

We'll wait upon your lordship.   55

Exeunt

[Much Ado About Nothing

Nothing

Act 2

4: **heartburned:** a pun. Don John is choleric (or hot under the collar), hence, he burns people with his fiery disposition.

8: **eldest son:** the favored or spoiled child

9: **tattling:** chattering

13-4: **shrewd of thy tongue:** Shrewish (or uncontrollable) women were said to talk too much.

Costume rendering for Beatrice from the 1958 production at the Shakespeare Memorial Theatre directed by Douglas Seale. See photographs from this production on pages 88, 172, and 260.

Photo: Rare Book and Special Collections Library, University of Illinois at Urbana-Champaign

Enter LEONATO, his brother [ANTHONIO],
his wife, HERO his daughter, and BEATRICE
his niece, and a KINSMAN

LEONATO
Was not Count John here at supper?

[ANTHONIO]
I saw him not.

BEATRICE
How tartly that gentleman looks. I never can see him but I am
heartburned an hour after.

HERO
He is of a very melancholy disposition.   5

BEATRICE
He were an excellent man that were made just in the midway
between him and Benedick. The one is too like an image and says
nothing, and the other too like my lady's eldest son, evermore
tattling.

LEONATO
Then half Signor Benedick's tongue in Count John's mouth, and   10
half Count John's melancholy in Signor Benedick's face–

BEATRICE
With a good leg and a good foot, uncle, and money enough in his
purse, such a man would win any woman in the world–if a could
get her goodwill.

LEONATO
By my troth, niece, thou wilt never get thee a husband, if thou be   15
so shrewd of thy tongue.

17: **she's too curst:** She has a difficult disposition; Beatrice follows with a play on the sense of being cursed by God.

19-20: **God sends a cursed cow...no horns:** There are two jokes intertwined here: (1) Only bulls have horns. Thus, Beatrice, a female, can never have horns. (2) The cuckold, a victim of female infidelity, was said to sprout horns. Again, since Beatrice is a female, no woman can be unfaithful to her, and thus she can never sprout horns.

24-25: **in the woollen:** between wool blankets. Shakespeare's father was in the wool trade.

32: **berrord...apes in hell:** "Berrord" is often modernized to read "bearherd" or "bear-herd," but as Horace Howard Furness (1899) pointed out, bears are not kept in flocks. Malone (1790) suggests that the bearherd might have been an animal trainer and keeper of some sort. Hence, he keeps bears and apes. William Warburton (1747) dismissed the idea of apes in hell as "impious nonsense." Shakespeare uses the same expression in *Taming of the Shrew*, 2.2.

34: **but:** only

35: **cuckold:** a victim of female infidelity, often depicted with horns on his head

[ANTHONIO]
In faith, she's too curst.

BEATRICE
Too curst is more than cursed. I shall lessen God's sending that
way, for it is said, God sends a cursed cow short horns, but to a
cow too curst he sends none.   20

LEONATO
So, by being too curst, God will send you no horns.

BEATRICE
Just, if he send me no husband, for the which blessing I am at him
upon my knees every morning and evening. Lord, I could not
endure a husband with a beard on his face. I had rather lie in the
woollen.   25

LEONATO
You may light on a husband that hath no beard.

BEATRICE
What should I do with him? Dress him in my apparel and make
him my waiting gentlewoman? He that hath a beard is more than
a youth, and he that hath no beard is less then a man, and he that
is more than a youth is not for me, and he that is less than a man,   30
I am not for him. Therefore, I will even take six pence in earnest
of the berrord and lead his apes into hell.

LEONATO
Well then, go you into hell.

BEATRICE
No, but to the gate, and there will the Devil meet me like an old
cuckold with horns on his head, and say, "Get you to heaven   35
Beatrice, get you to heaven. Here's no place for you maids." So
deliver I up my apes and away to Saint Peter 'fore the heavens.
He shows me where the bachelors sit, and there live we as merry
as the day is long.

41: make curtsy: make courtesy, or be polite; but Beatrice may also still be playing on the word "cursed"

48: clod: a lump of earth; **marl:** a kind of clay

49-50: Adam's sons...a sin to match my kindred: Since all men are descended from Adam, it would be incestuous to marry any of them.

53-61: The fault will be in the music...into his grave: puns on dancing and courtship. The passage also carries a suggestion that Beatrice is warning Hero not to be too easily seduced by the Prince's wooing.

56: jig: a dance associated with comedy

59: state and ancientry: what might be called pomp and circumstance, a mix of formality and fashion

60: his bad legs: hence, a bad dancer

60: cinque-pace: a popular dance, mentioned in Jehan Tabourot's *Art of Dancing* (1588)

62: apprehend: perceive; **passing:** extremely

63: church by daylight: perhaps something akin to "I have an eagle eye and am a good judge of character"

[ANTHONIO]
  [To HERO] Well niece, I trust you will be ruled by your father.   40

BEATRICE
  Yes, 'faith, it is my cousin's duty to make curtsy, and say, "Father,
  as it please you," but yet for all that, cousin, let him be a
  handsome fellow, or else make another cursty, and say, "Father, as
  it please me."

LEONATO
  Well niece, I hope to see you one day fitted with a husband.   45

BEATRICE
  Not till God make men of some other mettle than earth. Would it
  not grieve a woman to be overmastered with a piece of valiant
  dust, to make an account of her life to a clod of wayward marl?
  No, uncle, I'll none. Adam's sons are my brethren, and, truly, I
  hold it a sin to match in my kindred.   50

LEONATO
  Daughter, remember what I told you; if the Prince do solicit you
  in that kind, you know your answer.

BEATRICE
  The fault will be in the music, cousin, if you be not wooed in good
  time. If the Prince be too important, tell him there is measure in
  everything and so dance out the answer. For hear me, Hero,   55
  wooing, wedding, and repenting is as a Scotch jig, a measure, and
  a cinque-pace. The first suit is hot and hasty like a Scotch jig, and
  full as fantastical; the wedding, mannerly modest, as a measure
  full of state and ancientry; and then comes repentance, and with
  his bad legs falls into the cinque-pace faster and faster, till he sink   60
  into his grave.

LEONATO
  Cousin, you apprehend passing shrewdly.

BEATRICE
  I have a good eye, uncle. I can see a church by daylight.

64: Stage Direction: *BALTHAZAR and DON JOHN*: The quarto and folio read "*Balthasar, or dumbe Iohn*," but John is neither stupid nor silent. Malone (1790) and Collier (1853) suggested that someone read the text to the compositor, who heard "dumb" rather than "Don" or its variant "Dom." This solution, while ingenious, does not solve the problem of the conjunctive "or." This may be a sign of the quarto's inexact directions. For example, see 5.3.0's "*Enter CLAUDIO, DON PEDRO and three or four [ATTENDANTS] with tapers.*" Another solution is for Don John to be dressed as the murderous Balthazar from the then-famous *Spanish Tragedy* (1589) by Thomas Kyd. This creates some confusion since *Much Ado* also features the similarly named musician Balthasar who appears in 2.3. However, this confusion is limited only to readers, since Don John's disguise is never identified by any other character on stage.

65: "Lady, will you walk about with your friend?": Phoebe Cates as Hero and Brian Murray as Don Pedro in the New York Public Theater's 1987 production directed by Gerald Freedman

Photo: George E. Joseph

71-72: the lute should be like the case: Since everyone is in costume, Hero jokingly hopes that the face under the mask is a beautiful as the outward form.

73: Philemon, Jove: In Ovid's *Metamorphosis*, Baucis and Philemon received the gods Jupiter (Jove) and Mercury under their thatched hut; the book was a favorite of Shakespeare's.

76: Well, I would you did like me: This line was originally assigned to Benedick in the folio, but thereafter attributed to Balthasar. Editors follow Lewis Theobald (1733) in the reattribution.

LEONATO
    The revellers are entering. Brother, make good room.
        Enter DON PEDRO, CLAUDIO, and BENEDICK, BALTHASAR
        and DON JOHN, [BORACHIO, HERO, URSULA, MARGARET],
                        MASKERS with a drum

DON PEDRO
    Lady, will you walk about with your friend?   65

HERO
    So you walk softly and look sweetly and say nothing, I am yours
    for the walk, and especially when I walk away.

DON PEDRO
    With me in your company?

HERO
    I may say so when I please.

DON PEDRO
    And when please you to say so?   70

HERO
    When I like your favor, for God defend the lute should be like the
    case.

DON PEDRO
    My visor is Philemon's roof; within, the house is Jove.

HERO
    Why then your visor should be thatched.

DON PEDRO
    Speak low if you speak love.   75
                              [They step aside]

[BALTHASAR]
    Well, I would you did like me.

84: clerk: the parish clerk led the congregation in responses during church services

Kathleen Early as Hero and Dan Snook as Benedick in the Shakespeare Theatre Company's 2002-2003 production directed by Mark Lamos

Photo: Carol Rosegg

MARGARET
So would not I for your own sake, for I have many ill-qualities.

[BALTHASAR]
Which is one?

MARGARET
I say my prayers aloud.

[BALTHASAR]
I love you the better. The hearers may cry "Amen."   80

MARGARET
God match me with a good dancer.

BALTHASAR
Amen.

MARGARET
And God keep him out of my sight when the dance is done.
Answer, clerk.

BALTHASAR
No more words; the clerk is answered.   85
                                                   [They step aside]

URSULA
I know you well enough. You are Signor Anthonio.

ANTHONIO
At a word, I am not.

URSULA
I know you by the waggling of your head.

ANTHONIO
To tell you true, I counterfeit him.

91: **dry hand:** a sign of old age; young hands were supposed to be moist; **up and down:** in every detail

92: **At a word:** to be brief

94: **Mum:** i.e., stop arguing and be silent

95: **there's an end:** i.e., that's all

97: "No, you shall pardon me.": Judi Dench as Beatrice and Donald Sinden as Benedick in the 1976 RSC production directed by John Barton

Photo: Reg Wilson © Royal Shakespeare Company

100-101: *The Hundred Merry Tales:* according to Sheldon Zitner (1993), a collection of rude anecdotes published in 1526

URSULA
You could never do him so ill-well, unless you were the very man.   90
Here's his dry hand up and down. You are he, you are he.

ANTHONIO
At a word, I am not.

URSULA
Come, come, do you think I do not know you by your excellent
wit? Can virtue hide itself? Go to! Mum, you are he, graces will
appear, and there's an end.   95

[They step aside]

BEATRICE
Will you not tell me who told you so?

BENEDICK
No, you shall pardon me.

BEATRICE
Nor will you not tell me who you are?

BENEDICK
Not now.

BEATRICE
That I was disdainful, and that I had my good wit out of *The*   100
Hundred Merry Tales? Well, this was Signor Benedick that said so.

BENEDICK
What's he?

BEATRICE
I am sure you know him well enough.

BENEDICK
Not I, believe me.

BEATRICE
Did he never make you laugh?   105

107: Scene: Prince's jester: In 1788, John Philip Kemble's Benedick could not sit still while his Beatrice insulted him. He paced about "very much vexed...till, at last, he runs away...and she after him."

107: "Why, he is the Prince's Jester, a very dull fool.": Googie Withers as Beatrice and Michael Redgrave as Benedick in the 1958 RSC production directed by Douglas Seale
Photo: Angus McBean © Royal Shakespeare Company

108: impossible: unbelievable. Warburton (1747) suggested "impassable," an utterance which would not pass muster, but the quarto/folio reading works as is.

109: villainy: Beatrice refers to his immoral and impish nature, not necessarily an allusion to serious criminal behavior.

111: fleet: ships were often filled with convicts, hence villains; **boarded:** a sexual pun; Benedick is like a pirate, and she is a ship that he could have boarded; similarly used in *Taming of the Shrew* (1.5) and in *Othello* (1.2)

115: partridge wing: a tender piece of meat. Perhaps Beatrice is still playing on the sense of Benedick as a "stuffed man." She suggests here that it would not take much to fill his stomach. See 4.1.267, where Beatrice associates Benedick's renewed vows to food: "Will you not eat your word?"

BENEDICK
I pray you, what is he?

BEATRICE
Why, he is the Prince's jester, a very dull fool. Only his gift is in
devising impossible slanders. None but libertines delight in him,
and the commendation is not in his wit but in his villainy, for he
both pleases men and angers them, and then they laugh at him and   110
beat him. I am sure he is in the fleet. I would he had boarded me.

BENEDICK
When I know the gentleman, I'll tell him what you say.

BEATRICE
Do, do. He'll but break a comparison or two on me, which,
peradventure, not marked or not laughed at, strikes him into
melancholy. And then there's a partridge wing saved, for the fool   115
will eat no supper that night. We must follow the leaders.

BENEDICK
In every good thing.

BEATRICE
Nay, if they lead to any ill, I will leave them at the next turning.
                Exeunt [all but DON JOHN, BORACHIO, and CLAUDIO]
                                          Music for the dance

JOHN
Sure my brother is amorous on Hero and hath withdrawn her
father to break with him about it. The ladies follow her, and but   120
one visor remains.

BORACHIO
And that is Claudio, I know him by his bearing.

JOHN
[To CLAUDIO] Are not you Signor Benedick?

CLAUDIO
You know me well; I am he.

125: very near my bother in his love: a good friend of my brother. Most editions have John without costume, but in this line he identifies himself. Hence there is no reason to believe that does not enter the scene masked like the others.

127: birth: i.e., rank or status

137: all hearts...own tongues: In matters of love, each one should speak for himself.

139: agent: someone who works on your behalf

JOHN
Signor, you are very near my brother in his love. He is enamored   125
on Hero. I pray you dissuade him from her. She is no equal for his
birth. You may do the part of an honest man in it.

CLAUDIO
How know you he loves her?

JOHN
I heard him swear his affection.

BORACHIO
So did I too, and he swore he would marry her tonight.   130

JOHN
Come, let us to the banquet.

Exeunt all but CLAUDIO

CLAUDIO
Thus answer I in name of Benedick,
But hear these ill news with the ears of Claudio.
'Tis certain so. The Prince woos for himself.
Friendship is constant in all other things,   135
Save in the office and affairs of love.
Therefore all hearts in love use their own tongues;
Let every eye negotiate for itself
And trust no agent, for beauty is a witch
Against whose charms faith melteth into blood.   140
This is an accident of hourly proof,
Which I mistrusted not. Farewell, therefore, Hero.

Enter BENEDICK

BENEDICK
Count Claudio.

CLAUDIO
Yea, the same.

147: willow: emblem of a forsaken lover; **Count:** the quarto prints "county"

149: usurer's chain: a heavy chain and, thus, not easily forgotten or ignored

151: "I wish him joy of her.": Barrett Foa as Claudio in the Shakespeare Theatre Company's 2002-2003 production directed by Mark Lamos
Photo: Carol Rosegg

152: drover: shepherd of cattle. The imagery recalls Beatrice's bearherd (2.1.32).

156: 'Twas the boy...beat the post: The implication here is that Claudio has badly misinterpreted the facts. Furness (1899) suggests that the story of the blind man has a contemporary reference, but he can find no exact correspondence.

158: hurt fowl: poor, injured creature; **sedges:** reeds where birds may hide

163: Stage Direction: **Enter DON PEDRO:** The quarto prints "*Enter Prince, Hero, Leonato, Iohn and Borachio, and Conrade.*" but it is clear that Don John is not in this part of the scene. The folio merely has *Enter Prince.*

BENEDICK
Come, will you go with me?   145

CLAUDIO
Whither?

BENEDICK
Even to the next willow, about your own business, Count. What
fashion will you wear the garland of? About your neck, like an
usurer's chain? Or under your arm, like a lieutenant's scarf? You
must wear it one way, for the Prince hath got your Hero.   150

CLAUDIO
I wish him joy of her.

BENEDICK
Why that's spoken like an honest drover, so they sell bullocks!
But did you think the Prince would have served you thus?

CLAUDIO
I pray you, leave me.

BENEDICK
Ho! Now you strike like the blind man. 'Twas the boy that stole   155
your meat, and you'll beat the post.

CLAUDIO
If it will not be, I'll leave you.

Exit

BENEDICK
Alas, poor hurt fowl, now will he creep into sedges. But that my
lady Beatrice should know me, and not know me. The Prince's
fool! Hah? It may be I go under that title because I am merry. Yea.   160
But so I am apt to do myself wrong. I am not so reputed! It is the
base, though bitter, disposition of Beatrice that puts the world into
her person and so gives me out. Well, I'll be revenged as I may.
Enter [DON PEDRO]

166: **warren:** large game reserve; **lodge in a warren:** a lodger in an isolated cabin, hence lonely and depressed

169: **rod:** a bundle of twigs, used to beat children

172: **flat:** absolute, outright

DON PEDRO

Now Signor, where's the Count? Did you see him?

BENEDICK

Troth, my lord, I have played the part of Lady Fame. I found him   165
here as melancholy as a lodge in a warren. I told him and, I think
I told him true, that your Grace had got the goodwill of this young
lady, and I offered him my company to a willow tree, either to
make him a garland, as being forsaken, or to bind him up a rod as
being worthy to be whipped.   170

DON PEDRO

To be whipped? What's his fault?

BENEDICK

The flat transgression of a schoolboy, who, being overjoyed with
finding a bird's nest, shows it his companion, and he steals it.

DON PEDRO

Wilt thou make a trust a transgression? The transgression is in the
stealer.   175

BENEDICK

Yet it had not been amiss. The rod had been made, and the
garland too, for the garland he might have worn himself, and the
rod he might have bestowed on you, who, as I take it, have stolen
his bird's nest.

DON PEDRO

I will but teach them to sing and restore them to the owner.   180

BENEDICK

If their singing answer your saying, by my faith, you say honestly.

DON PEDRO

The Lady Beatrice hath a quarrel to you. The gentleman that
danced with her told her she is much wronged by you.

184: **misused:** insulted

187-188: **duller than a great thaw:** muddy, not clear

189: **conveyance:** dexterity

190: **poniards:** daggers

191: **terminations:** Beatrice's breath is so foul it kills or terminates. Alexander Dyce suggested "minations," (1859) Latin for "menace."

192: **to the North Star:** as far as the North Pole, or perhaps to the heavens

193: **marry her:** It is Benedick who first raises the possibility, suggesting that the Prince's task may not be all that difficult.

194-195: **Hercules have turned spit:** A.R. Humphreys (1981) refers to the classical legend of Omphale, who bought the enslaved Hercules from Hermes and forced him to work as a turnspit or spinner.

196: **Ate:** one of the Furies, Greek Goddess of Discord; mentioned in *Julius Caesar*: "With Ate by his side come hot from hell" (3.1); **in good apparel:** The Furies dress in rags.

200: Stage Direction: ***Enter...HERO:*** The quarto does not have her entering but the folio does.

200: Scene: In Edwin Booth's 1878 production Beatrice's entry was moved to just after Benedick's exit. The result was that his diatribe was rendered a public comic performance for his friends, not a serious speech meant to insult his one true love.

203: **Antipodes:** region on the furthest side of the earth

204: **tooth-picker:** Horace Howard Furness (1899) suggests that using a toothpick was a sign of elegance

205: **Prester John:** supposedly a Christian king of vast wealth who ruled a region of Asia

206: **Cham's beard:** Cham was king of the Mongols.

207: **pygmies:** not simply a race of short people, but, according to Marco Polo, a race derived from the monkeys of Sumatra

210: **Lady Tongue:** like Lady Disdain, a reference to an allegorical figure, hence the capitalization

BENEDICK

O, she misused me past the endurance of a block. An oak but with
one green leaf on it would have answered her! My very visor began   185
to assume life and scold with her! She told me, not thinking I had
been myself, that I was the Prince's jester, that I was duller than a
great thaw, huddling jest upon jest with such impossible
conveyance upon me that I stood like a man at a mark with a
whole army shooting at me. She speaks poniards, and every word   190
stabs. If her breath were as terrible as her terminations, there were
no living near her; she would infect to the North Star. I would not
marry her, though she were endowed with all that Adam had left
him before he transgressed. She would have made Hercules have
turned spit, yea, and have cleft his club to make the fire too. Come,   195
talk not of her. You shall find her the infernal Ate in good apparel.
I would to God some scholar would conjure her, for certainly while
she is, here a man may live as quiet in hell as in a sanctuary, and
people sin upon purpose because they would go thither; so indeed,
all disquiet, horror, and perturbation follows her.   200

Enter CLAUDIO and BEATRICE, LEONATO, [HERO]

DON PEDRO

Look, here she comes.

BENEDICK

Will your Grace command me any service to the world's end? I
will go on the slightest errand now to the Antipodes that you can
devise to send me on. I will fetch you a tooth-picker now from the
furthest inch of Asia, bring you the length of Prester John's foot,   205
fetch you a hair off the great Cham's beard, do you any embassage
to the pygmies, rather then hold three words' conference with this
harpy. You have no employment for me?

DON PEDRO

None, but to desire your good company.

BENEDICK

O God, sir, here's a dish I love not. I cannot endure my Lady Tongue.   210

Exit

215: put him down: embarrassed him publicly; used also in *Taming of the Shrew*, 5.2

224: civil...as an orange: a pun on civil and the city of Seville; part of the 1589 peace treaty between England and Spain was the annual delivery of Spanish marmalade made from oranges, grown in and around Seville

225: blazon: usually a proclamation, but here merely a judgment or statement

226: conceit: image of himself

227: broke with: negotiated with

Julia Marlow as Beatrice
By permission of Folger Shakespeare Library

DON PEDRO

Come, lady, come, you have lost the heart of Signor Benedick.

BEATRICE

Indeed, my lord, he lent it me a while, and I gave him use for it, a
double-heart for his single one. Marry, once before he won it of me
with false dice. Therefore, your Grace may well say I have lost it.

DON PEDRO

You have put him down, lady, you have put him down.   215

BEATRICE

So I would not he should do me, my lord, lest I should prove the
mother of fools. I have brought Count Claudio, whom you sent
me to seek.

DON PEDRO

Why how now Count, wherefore are you sad?

CLAUDIO

Not sad, my lord.   220

DON PEDRO

How then? Sick?

CLAUDIO

Neither, my lord.

BEATRICE

The Count is neither sad, nor sick, nor merry, nor well, but civil,
Count, civil as an orange, and something of that jealous complexion.

DON PEDRO

I'faith, lady, I think your blazon to be true, though I'll be sworn,   225
if he be so, his conceit is false. Here, Claudio, I have wooed in
thy name, and fair Hero is won. I have broke with her father
and his goodwill obtained. Name the day of marriage, and God
give thee joy.

tracks 11-13

230-256:
Budd Knapp as Leonato, Maureen Fitzgerald as Beatrice,
Bruce Armstrong as Claudio, and Ron Hastings as Don Pedro
David Bradley as Leonato, Saskia Reeves as Beatrice,
Jason O'Mara as Claudio, and Paul Jesson as Don Pedro

231: Grace hath...all grace: a pun of the Prince's title (your Grace) and saying grace

233: Silence is the perfectest herald of joy: My joy is beyond words.

239-240: windy side of care: Upwind, no predator can pick up your scent; thus, you are in no danger of being hunted.

242: Thus goes everyone to the world: i.e., everyone eventually gets married. Johnson (1765) suggested "to the wood."

243: sunburnt: "Sunburn" suggests a peasant who works out-of-doors. However, Beatrice is not single due to monetary concerns. We are later told that she would make an excellent wife for Benedick, and money (or the lack thereof) is not raised as an impediment. However, the Prince does suggest that Beatrice is not of royal blood. "Sunburnt" could also refer to a dark complexion, which, at the time, was not considered attractive.

243-244: "I may sit in a corner and cry, 'Heigh-ho for a husband.'": Julia Neilson as Beatrice from George Alexander's 1898 production at the St. James's Theatre (London)
By permission of the Folger Shakespeare Library

LEONATO

Count, take of me my daughter, and with her my fortunes. His   230
Grace hath made the match, and all grace say Amen to it.

BEATRICE

Speak, Count, 'tis your cue.

CLAUDIO

Silence is the perfectest herald of joy; I were but little happy if I
could say how much. Lady, as you are mine, I am yours. I give
away myself for you, and dote upon the exchange.   235

BEATRICE

Speak cousin, or, if you cannot, stop his mouth with a kiss and let
not him speak neither.

DON PEDRO

In faith, lady, you have a merry heart.

BEATRICE

Yea, my lord, I thank it. Poor fool, it keeps on the windy side of
care. My cousin tells him in his ear that he is in her heart.   240

CLAUDIO

And so she doth, cousin.

BEATRICE

Good Lord, for alliance. Thus goes everyone to the world but I,
and I am sunburnt. I may sit in a corner and cry, "Heigh-ho for a
husband."

DON PEDRO

Lady Beatrice, I will get you one.   245

BEATRICE

I would rather have one of your father's getting. Hath your Grace
ne'er a brother like you? Your father got excellent husbands, if a
maid could come by them.

tracks 11-13

230-256:
Budd Knapp as Leonato, Maureen Fitzgerald as Beatrice,
Bruce Armstrong as Claudio, and Ron Hastings as Don Pedro
David Bradley as Leonato, Saskia Reeves as Beatrice,
Jason O'Mara as Claudio, and Paul Jesson as Don Pedro

249: Scene: **Will you have me, lady:** Various productions have played with Don Pedro's proposal. The CBC Radio production (1962) has Ron Hasting's Don Pedro make the offer clearly in jest, while in the Public Theater's 1972 production, Douglass Watson's Don Pedro drops to his knees and proposes most seriously. Emma Thompson's Beatrice is not sure what to make of Denzel Washington's Don Pedro in Branagh's 1993 film. She is at first taken aback and then graciously sidesteps his offer.

255-6: **a star danced:** a star twinkled, a lucky sign

257: **those things:** not specifically explained, but whatever her task, it does serve to get her off stage

259: **pleasant, spirited:** sometimes printed as "pleasant-spirited"

262: **unhappiness:** Lewis Theobald (1733) suggested "an happiness," but this is unnecessary. Dreaming of something unpleasant, Beatrice reacts by laughing herself awake.

DON PEDRO

Will you have me, lady?

BEATRICE

No, my lord, unless I might have another for working days. Your   250
Grace is too costly to wear every day. But I beseech your Grace,
pardon me. I was born to speak all mirth, and no matter.

DON PEDRO

Your silence most offends me, and to be merry best becomes you,
for, out a question, you were born in a merry hour.

BEATRICE

No, sure my lord, my mother cried. But then there was a star   255
danced, and under that was I born. Cousins, God give you joy.

LEONATO

Niece, will you look to those things I told you of?

BEATRICE

I cry you mercy, uncle, by your Grace's pardon.

Exit BEATRICE.

DON PEDRO

By my troth, a pleasant, spirited lady.

LEONATO

There's little of the melancholy element in her, my lord. She is   260
never sad but when she sleeps and not ever sad then, for I have
heard my daughter say she hath often dreamt of unhappiness and
waked herself with laughing.

DON PEDRO

She cannot endure to hear tell of a husband.

LEONATO

O, by no means, she mocks all her wooers out of suit.   265

269: **Count:** the quarto prints "Countie"

270: **goes on crutches:** goes slowly

270: **love have all his rites:** "Love" here may be an invocation to Cupid.

272: **answer my mind:** arranged as I would wish

275: **Hercules' labors:** Hercules had to undertake twelve labors, each deadly.

277: **fain:** gladly

278: **minister:** provide me

280: **ten nights' watchings:** i.e., ten sleepless nights

DON PEDRO

She were an excellent wife for Benedick.

LEONATO

O Lord, my lord, if they were but a week married, they would talk
themselves mad.

DON PEDRO

Count Claudio, when mean you to go to church?

CLAUDIO

Tomorrow, my lord. Time goes on crutches, till love have all his rites. 270

LEONATO

Not till Monday, my dear son, which is hence a just sevennight,
and a time too brief too to have all things answer my mind.

DON PEDRO

Come, you shake the head at so long a breathing, but I warrant
thee, Claudio, the time shall not go dully by us. I will, in the
interim, undertake one of Hercules' labors, which is, to bring 275
Signor Benedick and the Lady Beatrice into a mountain of
affection, th' one with th' other. I would fain have it a match,
and I doubt not but to fashion it, if you three will but minister
such assistance as I shall give you direction.

LEONATO

My lord, I am for you, though it cost me ten nights' watchings. 280

CLAUDIO

And I, my lord.

DON PEDRO

And you too, gentle Hero?

HERO

I will do any modest office, my lord, to help my cousin to a good
husband.

285: **unhopefullest:** not without hope. The sense is that Benedick has what it takes to be a good husband.

286: **approved:** demonstrated

289: **practice on:** deceive

291: **Cupid, archer:** the son of Venus, Cupid wounds with amorous darts or arrows

293: **my drift:** what I am thinking

DON PEDRO

And Benedick is not the unhopefullest husband that I know. Thus 285
far can I praise him: he is of a noble strain, of approved valor, and
confirmed honesty. I will teach you how to humor your cousin
that she shall fall in love with Benedick, and I, with your two
helps, will so practice on Benedick that, in despite of his quick wit
and his queasy stomach, he shall fall in love with Beatrice. If we 290
can do this, Cupid is no longer an archer. His glory shall be ours,
for we are the only love gods. Go in with me, and I will tell you
my drift.

Exeunt

3: **medicinable:** medicinal

4: **sick in displeasure:** sick with hatred

5: **ranges evenly with:** parallels; **cross:** impede

7: **covertly:** secretly

10-11: **in the favor:** i.e., in the good graces

13: **at any unseasonable instant of the night:** very late at night

15: "What life is in that, to be the death of this marriage?": Glenn Fleshler as Don John and Michael Polak as Borachio in the Shakespeare Theatre Company's 2002-2003 production directed by Mark Lamos

Photo: Carol Rosegg

Act 2, Scene 2]

JOHN
It is so, the Count Claudio shall marry the daughter of Leonato.

BORACHIO
Yea, my lord, but I can cross it.

JOHN
Any bar, any cross, any impediment, will be medicinable to me.
I am sick in displeasure to him, and whatsoever comes athwart
his affection ranges evenly with mine. How canst thou cross this   5
marriage?

BORACHIO
Not honestly, my lord, but so covertly that no dishonesty shall
appear in me.

JOHN
Show me briefly how.

BORACHIO
I think I told your lordship a year since, how much I am in the   10
favor of Margaret, the waiting gentlewoman to Hero?

JOHN
I remember.

BORACHIO
I can, at any unseasonable instant of the night, appoint her to look
out at her lady's chamber window.

JOHN
What life is in that, to be the death of this marriage?   15

16: **temper:** create (by mixing ingredients)

19: **a contaminated stale:** a whore

21: **vex:** torment

23: **despite:** spite

25: **Intend:** pretend

28: **cozened:** cheated, deceived

32-33: Scene: **hear me call Margaret...term me Claudio:** Theobald (1733) rightly puzzles over why Margaret would call out Claudio's name. If Claudio were watching and assumed that Hero, making love to someone else, called out "Claudio," then Claudio should rightly suspect that someone was impersonating him. Hero, then, would be a victim, not a seductress. The second and third folio (1632 and 1663) substitute "Borachio" for "Claudio," though now he presumably has to explain to Margaret why she should call out his name though he calls out Hero's. Kenneth Branagh, in his 1993 film, solves the problem, first by staging the scene (it happens outside the text of the play), and then having Borachio, in sexual ecstasy, shout out "Hero" while Margaret remains silent.

35-6: **jealousy shall be called assurance:** jealousy will turn suspicion into certainty

38: Scene: **thy fee is a thousand ducats:** Don John offers no such reward in Branagh's Messina, a playground where all is free and plentiful.

39: **constant:** consistent, but also playing on the issue of Hero's constancy, which they are about to sully

41: **I will presently...day of marriage:** We have already learned that this is to be in a week or so, but apparently no one has told John.

BORACHIO

The poison of that lies in you to temper. Go you to the Prince your
brother, spare not to tell him that he hath wronged his honor in
marrying the renowned Claudio, whose estimation do you mightily
hold up, to a contaminated stale, such a one as Hero.

JOHN

What proof shall I make of that?   20

BORACHIO

Proof enough to misuse the Prince, to vex Claudio, to undo Hero
and kill Leonato. Look you for any other issue?

JOHN

Only to despite them, I will endeavor anything.

BORACHIO

Go then, find me a meet hour to draw Don Pedro and the Count
Claudio alone. Tell them that you know that Hero loves me. Intend a   25
kind of zeal both to the Prince and Claudio, as in love of your
brother's honor who hath made this match and his friend's
reputation, who is thus like to be cozened with the semblance of a
maid, that you have discovered thus. They will scarcely believe this
without trial. Offer them instances which shall bear no less likelihood   30
than to see me at her chamber window, hear me call Margaret "Hero,"
hear Margaret term me "Claudio," and bring them to see this the very
night before the intended wedding. For in the meantime I will so
fashion the matter that Hero shall be absent, and there shall appear
such seeming truth of Hero's disloyalty that jealousy shall be called   35
assurance, and all the preparation overthrown.

JOHN

Grow this to what adverse issue it can, I will put it in practice. Be
cunning in the working this, and thy fee is a thousand ducats.

BORACHIO

Be you constant in the accusation, and my cunning shall not
shame me.   40

JOHN

I will presently go learn their day of marriage.

Exeunt

5: **I am here already:** I'll be back before you know it.

6: Scene: *Exit*: The boy never returns. This may signal some sort of textual corruption or merely that Shakespeare forgot about him. In the BBC TV version (1984), the boy (Ben Losh) comes back to Benedick (Robert Lindsey) with a book, but, before the boy can address his lord, Benedick stops his mouth so as not to give away his hiding place. In the 1982 RSC production, the boy (Timothy Sullivan) repeatedly tries to give the book to Benedick (Derek Jacobi) in his various hiding places. Benedick shoos him away while the others pretend not to see him.

tracks 14-15

7-29:
Samuel West as Benedick

10: **argument:** subject

12: **drum and the fife, tabor and the pipe:** the drum and fife, instruments used in military marches; the tabor and pipe, instruments used on festive occasions

14: **good armor:** well-made suit of armor

15: **doublet:** a close-fitting body garment

16-17: **turned orthography:** i.e., became an orthographer, one who is concerned with correct or proper spelling

Act 2, Scene 3]

Enter BENEDICK [and BOY]

BENEDICK
Boy.

BOY.
Signor?

BENEDICK
In my chamber window lies a book; bring it hither to me in the orchard.

BOY.
I am here already sir.   5

BENEDICK
I know that, but I would have thee hence and here again.

Exit BOY

I do much wonder that one man, seeing how much another man is a fool when he dedicates his behaviors to love, will, after he hath laughed at such shallow follies in others, become the argument of his own scorn by falling in love. And such a man is   10
Claudio. I have known when there was no music with him but the drum and the fife, and now had he rather hear the tabor and the pipe; I have known when he would have walked ten mile afoot to see a good armor, and now will he lie ten nights awake carving the fashion of a new doublet; he was wont to speak plain and to the   15
purpose, like an honest man and a soldier; and now is he turned orthography. His words are a very fantastical banquet, just so many strange dishes. May I be so converted and see with these eyes? I cannot tell. I think not. I will not be sworn, but love may transform me to an oyster, but I'll take my oath on it, till he have   20
made an oyster of me, he shall never make me such a fool. One woman is fair, yet I am well; another is wise, yet I am well;

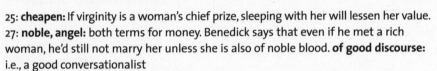

7-29:
Samuel West as Benedick

25: **cheapen:** If virginity is a woman's chief prize, sleeping with her will lessen her value.
27: **noble, angel:** both terms for money. Benedick says that even if he met a rich woman, he'd still not marry her unless she is also of noble blood. **of good discourse:** i.e., a good conversationalist
29: **Monsieur Love:** i.e., Claudio
29: Stage Direction: ***BALTHASAR:*** The folio refers here only to *Iacke Wilson*. Collier (1878) notes that Jack Wilson was a working musician of the era. The quarto has Balthasar entering at line 30, but most editions have him coming in with Don Pedro, Leonato, and Claudio.

33: "[Whispering] See you where Benedick hath hid himself?": Derek Jacobi as Benedick in the 1982 RSC production directed by Terry Hands
Photo: Joe Cocks © Shakespeare Birthplace Trust

35: **kid-fox:** young fox. Joseph Hanmer (1744) suggests "cade-fox" or "tame-fox." William Warburton (1747) suggests "hid-fox." Alexander Dyce (1857) leaves as is; **pennyworth:** a small amount. Perhaps the sense here is that a pennyworth will make him crave more.
37: **tax:** complain or blame
38: **To slander music anymore than once:** from the folio. The line is missing in the quarto.
41: **put a strange face:** downplay
42: **woo:** beg (you to play)

another virtuous, yet I am well. But till all graces be in one
woman, one woman shall not come in my grace. Rich she shall be,
that's certain; wise, or I'll none; virtuous, or I'll never cheapen   25
her; fair, or I'll never look on her; mild, or come not near me;
noble, or not I for an angel. Of good discourse, an excellent
musician, and her hair shall be of what color it please God. Hah!
The Prince and Monsieur Love, I will hide me in the arbor.

      Enter DON PEDRO, LEONATO, CLAUDIO and [BALTHASAR]

DON PEDRO
  Come, shall we hear this music?   30

CLAUDIO
  Yea, my good lord. How still the evening is.
  As hushed on purpose to grace harmony.

DON PEDRO
  [Whispering] See you where Benedick hath hid himself?

CLAUDIO
  [Whispering] O very well, my lord. The music ended,
  We'll fit the kid-fox with a pennyworth.   35

DON PEDRO
  Come, Balthasar, we'll hear that song again.

BALTHASAR
  O good, my lord, tax not so bad a voice
  To slander music any more than once.

DON PEDRO
  It is the witness still of excellency
  [To slander music anymore than once,]   40
  To put a strange face on his own perfection.
  I pray thee sing, and let me woo no more.

BALTHASAR
  Because you talk of wooing, I will sing–
  Since many a wooer doth commence his suit
  To her he thinks not worthy–yet he woos,   45
  Yet will he swear he loves–

47-48: if thou wilt...do it in notes: i.e., continue in song

50: crotchets: trifling arguments

52: air: i.e., song; **ravished:** carried away towards heaven

53: sheep's gut: used to make strings; **hale:** draw

55: Sigh no more: The song suggests that all men are inconstant; ironic, since it is Hero's, not Claudio's, virtue that will soon be questioned. Yet, Hero does remain constant in love; Claudio does not.

60: bonny: happy

63: ditties: love songs; **moe:** more

64: dumps: 1) low spirits, and 2) melancholy songs; **dull:** gloomy; **heavy:** sad

Costume rendering for Balthasar from the 1958 production at the Shakespeare Memorial Theatre directed by Douglas Seale. See photographs from this production on pages 88, 172, and 260.

Photo: Rare Book and Special Collections Library, University of Illinois at Urbana-Champaign

DON PEDRO

          Nay, pray thee, come,
Or if thou wilt hold longer argument,
Do it in notes.

BALTHASAR

          Note this before my notes.
There's not a note of mine that's worth the noting.

DON PEDRO

Why these are very crotchets that he speaks!   50
Note notes, forsooth, and nothing.

                      [BALTHASAR plays]

BENEDICK

Now divine air, now is his soul ravished. Is it not strange that
sheep's guts should hale souls out of men's bodies? Well, a horn
for my money when all's done.

BALTHASAR *[Singing]*

    Sigh no more ladies, sigh no more,   55
    Men were deceivers ever.
    One foot in sea, and one on shore,
    To one thing constant never.
    Then sigh not so, but let them go,
    And be you blithe and bonny,   60
    Converting all your sounds of woe,
    Into hey nonny nonny.
    Sing no more ditties, sing no moe,
    Of dumps so dull and heavy.
    The fraud of men was ever so,   65
    Since summer first was leafy.
    Then sigh not so, but let them go,
    And be you blithe and bonny,
    Converting all your sounds of woe,
    Into hey nonny nonny.   70

DON PEDRO

By my troth, a good song.

73: **shift:** a short spell

76: **lief:** from the folio, which corrects the quarto reading of "liue"; used also in *Taming of the Shrew* (1.1); **night-raven:** known for its ominous crowing. See *Macbeth*: "The raven himself is hoarse/ That croaks the fatal entrance of Duncan" (1.6).

79: **excellent music:** This planned serenade is quite forgotten. Again, this may suggest a cut in the promptbook, or that Shakespeare forgot, or that he chose not to include it for some reason.

83-128:
Paul Jesson as Don Pedro, David Bradley as Leonato,
Jason O'Mara as Claudio, and Samuel West as Benedick

tracks 16-17

85: **ay, stalk on, stalk on, the fowl sits:** i.e., keep hunting; he's almost caught

89: **ever to abhor:** As we see in 2.1.212-214, this is not so. Beatrice was evidently involved with Benedick once. Perhaps "ever" might here suggest something akin to "for the longest time."

90: **Sits the wind in that corner:** i.e., is that the way the wind is blowing?

BALTHASAR
And an ill singer, my lord.

DON PEDRO
Ha, no, no 'faith, thou sing'st well enough for a shift.

BENEDICK
An he had been a dog that should have howled thus, they would
have hanged him, and I pray God his bad voice bode no mischief.   75
I had as liefe have heard the night-raven, come what plague could
have come after it.

DON PEDRO
Yea, marry, dost thou hear Balthasar? I pray thee get us some
excellent music, for tomorrow night we would have it at the Lady
Hero's chamber window.   80

BALTHASAR
The best I can, my lord.

DON PEDRO
Do so, farewell.

Exit Balthasar.
Come hither Leonato. What was it you told me of today, that your
niece Beatrice was in love with Signor Benedick?

CLAUDIO
[*Whispering*] O ay, stalk on, stalk on, the fowl sits. [*Aloud*] I did   85
never think that lady would have loved any man.

LEONATO
No, nor I neither, but most wonderful that she should so dote on
Signor Benedick, whom she hath in all outward behaviors seemed
ever to abhor.

BENEDICK
Is't possible? Sits the wind in that corner?   90

tracks 16-17

83-128:
Paul Jesson as Don Pedro, David Bradley as Leonato,
Jason O'Mara as Claudio, and Samuel West as Benedick

91-92: "But that she loves him with an enraged affection, it is past the infinite of thought.": Donald Sinden as Benedick in the 1976 RSC production directed by John Barton

Photo: Reg Wilson © Royal Shakespeare Company

92: **enraged affection:** wild abandon

92-93: **past the infinite of thought:** beyond measure

93: **counterfeit:** pretend

96: **discovers:** reveals to others who see her

100: **sit you:** sit with you

106: **gull:** joke; **white-bearded fellow:** i.e., Don Pedro

107: **Knavery:** duplicity

LEONATO

By my troth, my lord, I cannot tell what to think of it. But that
she loves him with an enraged affection, it is past the infinite of
thought.

DON PEDRO

Maybe she doth but counterfeit.

CLAUDIO

'Faith, like enough.

LEONATO

O God! Counterfeit? There was never counterfeit of passion came   95
so near the life of passion as she discovers it.

DON PEDRO

Why, what effects of passion shows she?

CLAUDIO

[Whispering] Bait the hook well; this fish will bite.

LEONATO

What effects, my lord? She will sit you—you heard my daughter   100
tell you how.

CLAUDIO

She did indeed.

DON PEDRO

How, how I pray you? You amaze me! I would have thought her
spirit had been invincible against all assaults of affection.

LEONATO

I would have sworn it had, my lord, especially against Benedick.   105

BENEDICK

I should think this a gull, but that the white-bearded fellow
speaks it. Knavery cannot sure hide himself in such reverence.

tracks 16-17

>83-128:
Paul Jesson as Don Pedro, David Bradley as Leonato,
Jason O'Mara as Claudio, and Samuel West as Benedick

115: **smock:** slip or other similar undergarment

118: **us of:** from the folio; the quarto reads "of us"

120: **between the sheet:** suggestive of being in bed together

121: **That:** Capell (1768) suggests that "That" be placed at the end of Leonato's speech, though it's not necessary. Perhaps Claudio means, "Oh, that story! I know it well."

122: **into a thousand halfpence:** into small pieces

124: **flout:** reject

127: **prays:** Collier (1853) suggests "cries"

CLAUDIO

[Whispering] He hath ta'en th' infection; hold it up.

DON PEDRO

Hath she made her affection known to Benedick?

LEONATO

No, and swears she never will. That's her torment. 110

CLAUDIO

'Tis true indeed, so your daughter says. "Shall I," says she, "that have so oft encountered him with scorn, write to him that I love him?"

LEONATO

This says she now when she is beginning to write to him, for she'll be up twenty times a night, and there will she sit in her smock, till 115 she have writ a sheet of paper. My daughter tells us all.

CLAUDIO

Now you talk of a sheet of paper, I remember a pretty jest your daughter told us of.

LEONATO

O! When she had writ it and was reading it over, she found Benedick and Beatrice between the sheet. 120

CLAUDIO

That.

LEONATO

O, she tore the letter into a thousand halfpence, railed at herself, that she should be so immodest to write to one that she knew would flout her. "I measure him," says she, "by my own spirit, for I should flout him if he writ to me, yea though I love him, I should." 125

CLAUDIO

Then down upon her knees she falls, weeps, sobs, beats her heart, tears her hair, prays, curses, "O sweet Benedick, God give me patience!"

129: **ecstasy:** madness

130: **overborne:** overcome

136: **alms:** that which is given in charity (alms were given out by the church). The sense here is: "It would be a blessing (to Beatrice) if Benedick were dead; at least then Beatrice would be free of the torment of his love."

138-139: "And she is exceeding wise. / In everything, but in loving Benedick.": Kevin Kline as Benedick in the New York Public Theater's 1987 production directed by Gerald Freedman
Photo: George E. Joseph

140: **blood:** passion

143: **dotage:** distraction or desperation; **daft:** put aside. The Prince suggests that he would have married her (perhaps to further enhance Beatrice in Benedick's eyes).

LEONATO

    She doth indeed, my daughter says so, and the ecstasy hath so
    much overborne her that my daughter is sometime afeared she   130
    will do a desperate outrage to herself. It is very true.

DON PEDRO

    It were good that Benedick knew of it by some other, if she will
    not discover it.

CLAUDIO

    To what end? He would make but a sport of it and torment the
    poor lady worse.   135

DON PEDRO

    An he should, it were an alms to hang him! She's an excellent,
    sweet lady, and, out of all suspicion, she is virtuous.

CLAUDIO

    And she is exceeding wise.

DON PEDRO

    In everything, but in loving Benedick.

LEONATO

    O, my lord, wisdom and blood, combating in so tender a body, we   140
    have ten proofs to one that blood hath the victory. I am sorry for
    her, as I have just cause, being her uncle and her guardian.

DON PEDRO

    I would she had bestowed this dotage on me. I would have daft
    all other respects and made her half myself. I pray you, tell
    Benedick of it and hear what a will say.   145

LEONATO

    Were it good, think you?

149: **bate:** abate, subside

154: **proper:** George Steevens (1773) suggests Claudio means "handsome."

155: **He hath...outward happiness:** He is good looking and perhaps also possesses a good disposition.

159: **Hector:** brave prince of Troy

165: **large:** James O. Halliwell-Phillips (1848) suggests the Prince means "free" or "licentious," but more likely the meaning here is "well known" or "public."

CLAUDIO

Hero thinks surely she will die, for she says she will die if he love her not, and she will die ere she make her love known, and she will die if he woo her, rather than she will bate one breath of her accustomed crossness.   150

DON PEDRO

She doth well. If she should make tender of her love 'tis very possible he'll scorn it, for the man, as you know all, hath a contemptible spirit.

CLAUDIO

He is a very proper man.

DON PEDRO

He hath indeed a good outward happiness.   155

CLAUDIO

Before God, and in my mind, very wise.

DON PEDRO

He doth indeed show some sparks that are like wit.

LEONATO

And I take him to be valiant.

DON PEDRO

As Hector, I assure you, and in the managing of quarrels you may say he is wise, for either he avoids them with great discretion, or   160
undertakes them with a most Christian-like fear.

LEONATO

If he do fear God, he must necessarily keep peace; if he break the peace, he ought to enter into a quarrel with fear and trembling.

DON PEDRO

And so will he do, for the man doth fear God, howsoever it seems not in him by some large jests he will make. Well, I am sorry for   165
your niece. Shall we go seek Benedick and tell him of her love?

168: "She may wear her heart out first.": Roger Allam as Benedick, John McAndrew as Claudio, John Carlisle as Don Pedro, and Leonato as Paul Webster in the 1990 RSC production directed by Bill Alexander

Photo: Joe Cocks © Shakespeare Birthplace Trust

171-172: **unworthy to have so good a lady:** from the folio. The quarto prints "unworthy so good a lady."

180: **dumb show:** a form of mime theater. Don Pedro says that the normally talkative couple will be tongue-tied, or as silent as a dumb show.

181: **sadly borne:** conveyed seriously

181-213
Sir John Gielgud as Benedick and Dame Peggy Ashcroft as Beatrice

183: **her affections have their full bent:** Cupid's bow is fully bent, ready to be fired.

184: **censured:** ridiculed

190: **reprove it:** dispute it

CLAUDIO
Never tell him, my lord. Let her wear it out with good counsel.

LEONATO
Nay, that's impossible! She may wear her heart out first.

DON PEDRO
Well, we will hear further of it by your daughter. Let it cool the
while. I love Benedick well, and I could wish he would modestly   170
examine himself to see how much he is unworthy to have so good
a lady.

LEONATO
My Lord, will you walk? Dinner is ready.

CLAUDIO
[Whispering] If he do not dote on her upon this, I will never trust
my expectation.   175

DON PEDRO
[Whispering] Let there be the same net spread for her, and that
must your daughter and her gentlewomen carry. The sport will
be, when they hold one an opinion of another's dotage, and no
such matter. That's the scene that I would see, which will be
merely a dumb show. Let us send her to call him into dinner.   180

Exeunt all but BENEDICK

BENEDICK
This can be no trick. The conference was sadly borne; they have
the truth of this from Hero. They seem to pity the lady. It seems
her affections have their full bent. Love me? Why it must be
requited. I hear how I am censured. They say I will bear myself
proudly, if I perceive the love come from her; they say, too, that   185
she will rather die than give any sign of affection. I did never
think to marry. I must not seem proud. Happy are they that hear
their detractions and can put them to mending. They say the lady
is fair; 'tis a truth, I can bear them witness. And virtuous, 'tis so,
I cannot reprove it. And wise, but for loving me—by my troth, it is   190
no addition to her wit, nor no great argument of her folly, for I will

181-213
Sir John Gielgud as Benedick and Dame Peggy Ashcroft as Beatrice

193: **broken on me:** insulted at my expense

196: **paper bullets:** hurtful insults

197: **career:** course; **humor:** inclination

197: Scene: **No, the world must be peopled:** The drama critic Leigh Hunt recalled that Charles Kemble, who first played the part in 1803, uttered this line "with his hands linked behind him, a general elevation of his aspect, and a sort of look at the whole universe before him, as if he saw all the future depended on his verdict..." In 1969, Alan Howard shouted the line while smashing his gardener's hat between his fists.

207: **daw:** jackdaw, a kind of crow; **no stomach:** no appetite

212: **Jew:** Shakespeare may be suggesting here that non-Christians were without religious faith. Hence, if Benedick were Jewish, he would be a faithless or inconstant lover.

be horribly in love with her. I may chance have some odd quirks
and remnants of wit broken on me, because I have railed so long
against marriage. But doth not the appetite alter? A man loves the
meat in his youth that he cannot endure in his age. Shall quips   195
and sentences and these paper bullets of the brain awe a man
from the career of his humor? No, the world must be peopled.
When I said I would die a bachelor, I did not think I should live
till I were married. Here comes Beatrice. By this day, she's a fair
lady! I do spy some marks of love in her.   200

Enter BEATRICE

BEATRICE
Against my will, I am sent to bid you come in to dinner.

BENEDICK
Fair Beatrice, I thank you for your pains.

BEATRICE
I took no more pains for those thanks than you take pains to
thank me. If it had been painful, I would not have come.

BENEDICK
You take pleasure, then, in the message?   205

BEATRICE
Yea, just so much as you may take upon a knife's point and choke
a daw withal. You have no stomach, signor, fare you well.

Exit

BENEDICK
Ha! "Against my will I am sent to bid you come into dinner."
There's a double meaning in that. "I took no more pains for those
thanks than you took pains to thank me." That's as much as to   210
say, "Any pains that I take for you is as easy as thanks." If I do not
take pity of her I am a villain; if I do not love her I am a Jew. I
will go get her picture.

Exit

[Much Ado About
Nothing

Act 3

0: Stage Direction: **_URSULA:_** from the folio; the quarto reads "_Urseley_"

3: **Proposing:** conversing

7: **pleached bower:** thick hedge of intertwining branches; thus, a place where Beatrice can hide

9-10: **favorites...princes:** ministers or perhaps just hangers-on

16: **trace:** pace

20-21: "My talk to thee must be how Benedick / Is sick in love with Beatrice": Fay Davis as Hero from George Alexander's 1898 production at the St. James's Theatre (London)

By permission of the Folger Shakespeare Library

24: **lapwing:** a plover, a bird known for its cunning and protection of its young

Act 3, Scene 1]

Enter HERO and two [GENTLEWOMEN],
MARGARET, and [URSULA]

HERO
Good Margaret, run thee to the parlor.
There shalt thou find my cousin Beatrice
Proposing with the Prince and Claudio.
Whisper her ear and tell her I and Ursula
Walk in the orchard and our whole discourse   5
Is all of her. Say that thou overheardst us,
And bid her steal into the pleached bower,
Where honeysuckles, ripened by the sun,
Forbid the sun to enter, like favorites
Made proud by princes that advance their pride   10
Against that power that bred it. There will she hide her
To listen our propose. This is thy office,
Bear thee well in it, and leave us alone.

MARGARET
I'll make her come, I warrant you, presently.

HERO
Now Ursula, when Beatrice doth come,   15
As we do trace this alley up and down,
Our talk must only be of Benedick.
When I do name him, let it be thy part
To praise him more then ever man did merit.
My talk to thee must be how Benedick   20
Is sick in love with Beatrice; of this matter
Is little Cupid's crafty arrow made,
That only wounds by hearsay. *[Whispering]* Now begin,
For look where Beatrice, like a lapwing, runs
Close by the ground to hear our conference.   25
Enter BEATRICE

26: **angling:** fishing

27: **golden oars:** i.e., a fish's fins

30: **couched:** hidden; **woodbine coverture:** a shelter or screen of honeysuckle (woodbine)

35: **coy:** disdainful

36: **haggards:** wild female hawks or falcons, captured but never fully tamed. The inference here is that the wild Beatrice is about to be ensnared.

36-37: "But are you sure / That Benedick loves Beatrice so entirely?": Celia Madeoy as Ursula, Kathleen Early as Hero, and Karen Ziemba as Beatrice in the Shakespeare Theatre Company's 2002-2003 production directed by Mark Lamos
Photo: Carol Rosegg

38: **new-trothed:** newly betrothed

46: **couch:** lie

URSULA

    [Whispering] The pleasant'st angling is to see the fish
    Cut with her golden ores the silver stream
    And greedily devour the treacherous bait.
    So angle we for Beatrice, who even now
    Is couched in the woodbine coverture.   30
    Fear you not my part of the dialogue.

HERO

    [Whispering] Then go we near her that her ear lose nothing
    Of the false, sweet bait that we lay for it.
    [Aloud] No truly Ursula, she is too disdainful;
    I know her spirits are as coy and wild   35
    As haggards of the rock.

URSULA

                  But are you sure
    That Benedick loves Beatrice so entirely?

HERO

    So says the Prince and my new-trothed lord.

URSULA

    And did they bid you tell her of it, madam?

HERO

    They did entreat me to acquaint her of it,   40
    But I persuaded them, if they loved Benedick,
    To wish him wrestle with affection
    And never to let Beatrice know of it.

URSULA

    Why did you so? Doth not the gentleman
    Deserve as full as fortunate a bed   45
    As ever Beatrice shall couch upon?

49: **framed:** designed
52: **Misprizing:** downplaying. Johnson (1765) suggests the meaning here is "despising."
55: **project:** projection, image

57-58: "And therefore certainly it were not good / She knew his love, lest she'll make sport at it.": Kristen Johnston as Beatrice, Elizabeth Waterston as Hero, Jane Houdyshell as Ursula, and Peter McCain and Bill Heck as attendants in The Public Theater 2004 production directed by David Esbjornson
Photo: Michal Daniel

60: **How:** however
61: **spell him backward:** describe him in a perverse or opposite way (with the effect of turning love to hate)
63: **black:** Malone (1790) suggests swarthy or dark brown, but the sense here is the darkly serious versus the *antic* or foolish; **Nature:** here, deified; **antic:** fantastic or foolish figure
64: **lance:** spear; **ill-headed:** The lance's point is flawed or defective in some way.
65: **low:** short; **an agate:** like the little figure cut into an agate stone, a stone often set into a ring
66: **vane:** weather vane
71: **carping:** complaining, insulting
72: **from all fashions:** unlike the accepted mode of behavior

HERO
 O god of love! I know he doth deserve
 As much as may be yielded to a man,
 But Nature never framed a woman's heart
 Of prouder stuff than that of Beatrice.   50
 Disdain and scorn ride sparkling in her eyes,
 Misprizing what they look on, and her wit
 Values itself so highly that to her
 All matter else seems weak. She cannot love,
 Nor take no shape nor project of affection,   55
 She is so self-endeared.

URSULA
      Sure I think so,
 And therefore certainly it were not good
 She knew his love, lest she'll make sport at it.

HERO
 Why you speak truth, I never yet saw man,
 How wise, how noble, young, how rarely featured,   60
 But she would spell him backward. If fair-faced,
 She would swear the gentleman should be her sister;
 If black, why Nature, drawing of an antic,
 Made a foul blot; if tall, a lance ill-headed;
 If low, an agate very vilely cut;   65
 If speaking, why a vane blown with all winds;
 If silent, why a block moved with none.
 So turns she every man the wrong side out,
 And never gives to truth and virtue that
 Which simpleness and merit purchaseth.   70

URSULA
 Sure, sure, such carping is not commendable.

HERO
 No, not to be so odd and from all fashions
 As Beatrice is, cannot be commendable,
 But who dare tell her so? If I should speak,
 She would mock me into air. O, she would laugh me 75

76: press me to death: allusion to an ancient torture or punishment

84: honest: chaste; **honest slanders:** malicious gossip that does not impugn modesty or chastity

85: stain: ruin

95-97: "Signor Benedick, / For shape, for bearing argument and valor, / Goes foremost in report through Italy.": Helen Mirren as Hero, Janet Suzman as Beatrice, and Rowena Cooper as Ursula in the 1968 RSC production directed by Trevor Nunn
Photo: Tom Holte © Shakespeare Birthplace Trust

96: bearing argument: manner of discussion and debate

Out of myself, press me to death with wit.
Therefore, let Benedick, like covered fire,
Consume away in sighs, waste inwardly.
It were a better death to die with mocks,
Which is as bad as die with tickling.   80

URSULA
Yet tell her of it; hear what she will say.

HERO
No, rather I will go to Benedick
And counsel him to fight against his passion,
And, truly, I'll devise some honest slanders
To stain my cousin with. One doth not know   85
How much an ill word may empoison liking.

URSULA
O, do not do your cousin such a wrong!
She cannot be so much without true judgment,
Having so swift and excellent a wit
As she is prized to have, as to refuse   90
So rare a gentleman as Signor Benedick.

HERO
He is the only man of Italy,
Always excepted my dear Claudio.

URSULA
I pray you, be not angry with me, madam,
Speaking my fancy. Signor Benedick,   95
For shape, for bearing argument and valor,
Goes foremost in report through Italy.

HERO
Indeed, he hath an excellent good name.

URSULA
His excellence did earn it ere he had it.
When are you married, madam?   100

104: **limed:** caught; birds were trapped with a sticky substance, bird-lime

106: **haps:** chance, happenstance

tracks 20-22

108-117
Maureen Fitzgerald as Beatrice
Pauline Jameson as Beatrice

111: **behind the back:** Collier (1853) suggested "but in the lack." However, the following reading can be made as is: Beatrice recognizes (hence "sees the backs of") that "contempt" and "maiden pride" will not get her far.

113: **Taming...loving hand:** Picking up on the image of wild hawks or falcons, Beatrice asks Benedick to tame her; part of a image cluster dealing with birds (see 3.1.36).

117: **reportingly:** as it is reported

HERO

    Why every day tomorrow. Come go in,
    I'll show thee some attires and have thy counsel,
    Which is the best to furnish me tomorrow.

URSULA

    [Whispering] She's limed, I warrant you. We have caught her,
    madam!   105

HERO .

    If it prove so, then loving goes by haps,
    Some Cupid kills with arrows, some with traps.

                                                 [Exeunt all but BEATRICE]

BEATRICE

    What fire is in mine ears? Can this be true?
    Stand I condemned for pride and scorn so much?
    Contempt, farewell, and maiden pride, adieu;   110
    No glory lives behind the back of such.
    And Benedick, love on, I will requite thee,
    Taming my wild heart to thy loving hand.
    If thou dost love, my kindness shall incite thee
    To bind our loves up in a holy band.   115
    For others say thou dost deserve, and I
    Believe it better than reportingly.

                                                 Exit

1: **consummate:** consummated

3: **vouchsafe:** allow

4: **soil:** stain

8: **hangman:** a term of endearment, perhaps akin to "rogue"

16: **toothache:** a sign of lovesickness; see Fletcher and Massinger's *The False One* (1620): "You had best be troubled with the tooth-ache too, For lovers ever are" (II.iii.p.254, ed. Alexander Dyce)

16: "I have the toothache.": Clive Merrison as Benedick in the 1988 RSC production directed by Di Trevis

Photo: Reg Wilson © Royal Shakespeare Company

Enter DON PEDRO, CLAUDIO, BENEDICK, and LEONATO

DON PEDRO
I do but stay till your marriage be consummate, and then go I
toward Aragon.

CLAUDIO
I'll bring you thither, my lord, if you'll vouchsafe me.

DON PEDRO
Nay, that would be as great a soil in the new gloss of your
marriage as to show a child his new coat and forbid him to wear   5
it; I will only be bold with Benedick for his company, for, from the
crown of his head to the sole of his foot, he is all mirth. He hath
twice or thrice cut Cupid's bowstring, and the little hangman
dare not shoot at him. He hath a heart as sound as a bell, and his
tongue is the clapper, for what his heart thinks, his tongue speaks.   10

BENEDICK
Gallants, I am not as I have been.

LEONATO
So say I, methinks you are sadder.

CLAUDIO
I hope he be in love.

DON PEDRO
Hang him truant, there's no true drop of blood in him to be truly
touched with love. If he be sad, he wants money.   15

BENEDICK
I have the toothache.

19: hang it...afterwards: playing on hangman. The tooth is drawn and quartered, as is a criminal during execution.

21: worm: In *Of the Teeth* (1582), we learn that toothaches are caused by worms who breed in the cheek.

23: "Yet, say I, he is in love.": Barrett Foa as Claudio, Dan Snook as Benedick, Peter Rini as Don Pedro, and Michael Santo as Leonato in the Shakespeare Theatre Company's 2002-2003 production directed by Mark Lamos
Photo: Carol Rosegg

24: no appearance of fancy in him: no obvious signs of love

25-28: strange disguises...no doublet: odd and, in this case, fashionable clothes from Holland, France, Germany, and Spain.

27: slops: pants

28: fancy: sudden desire

31-32: old signs: conventional or tell-tale signs

34-35: old ornament of his cheek: i.e., his previous beard

35: stuffed tennis balls: Tennis balls were traditionally stuffed with hair bought from barbers.

DON PEDRO
Draw it.

BENEDICK
Hang it.

CLAUDIO
You must hang it first and draw it afterwards.

DON PEDRO
What? Sigh for the toothache?   20

LEONATO
Where is but a humor or a worm.

BENEDICK
Well, everyone cannot master a grief, but he that has it.

CLAUDIO
Yet, say I, he is in love.

DON PEDRO
There is no appearance of fancy in him, unless it be a fancy that he
hath to strange disguises, as to be a Dutchman today, a Frenchman   25
tomorrow, or in the shape of two countries at once, as a German
from the waist downward, all slops, and a Spaniard from the hip
upward, no doublet. Unless he have a fancy to this foolery, as it
appears he hath, he is no fool for fancy, as you would have it
appear he is.   30

CLAUDIO
If he be not in love with some woman, there is no believing old
signs: a brushes his hat o' mornings—what should that bode?

DON PEDRO
Hath any man seen him at the barber's?

CLAUDIO
No, but the barber's man hath been seen with him, and the old
ornament of his cheek hath already stuffed tennis balls.   35

36: Scene: **Indeed....loss of a beard:** In the RSC (1991), Roger Allam sat in a chair with a white towel over his face, which was pulled off here to reveal his newly shaven face.

37: **civit:** perfume

43: **lute-string:** Lutes are instruments associated with wooing and love-songs.

44: **stops:** frets of the lute's neck

45: **heavy:** serious

49: **yes...dies for him:** Though Benedick is rather unlovable, Beatrice is lovesick for him.

50: **face upwards:** Theobald (1733) queried: "Are not all men and women buried so?" He suggested that "upwards" be changed to "downwards." But as Malone (1790) made clear, the point is not the positioning of the body; merely that Beatrice is likely to die for love of Benedick. Claire McEachern (2006) suggests the phrase refers to a woman covered by a man in the act of coitus.

LEONATO
Indeed, he looks younger than he did, by the loss of a beard.

DON PEDRO
Nay a rubs himself with civit. Can you smell him out by that?

CLAUDIO
That's as much as to say, the sweet youth's in love.

DON PEDRO
The greatest note of it is his melancholy.

CLAUDIO
And when was he wont to wash his face?   40

DON PEDRO
Yea, or to paint himself? For the which I hear what they say of
him.

CLAUDIO
Nay, but his jesting spirit, which is now crept into a lute-string,
and now governed by stops.

DON PEDRO
Indeed, that tells a heavy tale for him. Conclude, conclude: he is   45
in love.

CLAUDIO
Nay, but I know who loves him.

DON PEDRO
That would I know too. I warrant one that knows him not.

CLAUDIO
Yes, and his ill-conditions and, in despite of all, dies for him.

DON PEDRO
She shall be buried with her face upwards.   50

51: **charm:** magic cure

53: **hobbyhorses:** immature jesters, buffoons

54: **break with him:** consult with him

59: **Good den:** short for "God give you good evening"

Glenn Fleshler as Don John in the Shakespeare Theatre Company's 2002-2003 production directed by Mark Lamos

Photo: Carol Rosegg

BENEDICK

Yet is this no charm for the toothache. *[To Leonato]* Old signor,
walk aside with me. I have studied eight or nine wise words to
speak to you, which these hobbyhorses must not hear.

[BENEDICK and LEONATO exit]

DON PEDRO

For my life, to break with him about Beatrice.

CLAUDIO

'Tis even so. Hero and Margaret have by this played their parts   55
with Beatrice, and then the two bears will not bite one another
when they meet.

Enter JOHN THE BASTARD

JOHN

My lord and brother, God save you.

DON PEDRO

Good den brother.

JOHN

If your leisure served, I would speak with you.   60

DON PEDRO

In private?

JOHN

If it please you, yet Count Claudio may hear, for what I would
speak of concerns him.

DON PEDRO

What's the matter?

JOHN

[To CLAUDIO] Means your lordship to be married tomorrow?   65

DON PEDRO

You know he does.

68: **discover:** reveal

69-70: **aim better at me:** judge my character more accurately

74: **circumstances shortened:** i.e., to get right to the point

75: **disloyal:** unfaithful

75: Scene: **The lady is disloyal:** In the BBC TV version, on Don John's uttering of this line, Claudio (played by Robert Reynolds) threw a cup of wine in Don John's face.

79: **paint out:** describe

85: **May:** can

JOHN
I know not that, when he knows what I know.

CLAUDIO
If there be any impediment, I pray you discover it.

JOHN
You may think I love you not. Let that appear hereafter and aim
better at me by that I now will manifest. For my brother, I think   70
he holds you well and in dearness of heart hath holp to effect your
ensuing marriage. Surely suit ill-spent and labor ill-bestowed.

DON PEDRO
Why, what's the matter?

JOHN
I came hither to tell you, and, circumstances shortened, for she
has been too long a talking of. The lady is disloyal.   75

CLAUDIO
Who, Hero?

JOHN
Even she, Leonato's Hero, your Hero, every man's Hero.

CLAUDIO
Disloyal?

JOHN
The word is too good to paint out her wickedness. I could say she
were worse. Think you of a worse title, and I will fit her to it.   80
Wonder not till further warrant. Go but with me tonight. You
shall see her chamber window entered, even the night before her
wedding day. If you love her then, tomorrow wed her, but it
would better fit your honor to change your mind.

CLAUDIO
May this be so?   85

94-95: **Bear it coldly:** stay calm

95: **let the issue show itself:** i.e., let the issue be resolved by what you see

96: **untowardly:** unluckily; with likelihood or suggestion of misfortune or mishap

97: **strangely:** extraordinarily, surprisingly

DON PEDRO
I will not think it.

JOHN
If you dare not trust that you see, confess not that you know. If
you will follow me, I will show you enough, and when you have
seen more and heard more, proceed accordingly.

CLAUDIO
If I see anything tonight why I should not marry her, tomorrow,   90
in the congregation, where I should wed, there will I shame her.

DON PEDRO
And as I wooed for thee to obtain her, I will join with thee to
disgrace her.

JOHN
I will disparage her no farther, till you are my witnesses. Bear it
coldly but till midnight, and let the issue show itself.   95

DON PEDRO
O day untowardly turned!

CLAUDIO
O mischief strangely thwarting!

JOHN
O plague right well prevented! So will you say, when you have
seen the sequel.

[Exeunt]

tracks 23-25

1-23
William Fulton as Dogberry and Roger Crowther as Verges
Bryan Pringle as Dogberry, Raymond Bowers as Verges,
Alisdair Simpson as First Watch, and Chris Pavlo as Second Watch

0: Scene: David Waller's Dogberry (1968) was described by Gareth Lloyd Evans as "a triumph—he moves like a red balloon which is never quite pricked and his comic business has the blessing of economy." The BBC TV version featured Michael Eliphick as a working-class constable who aspires to rubbing shoulders with his social superiors. The recent Spartan Theater production (2002) loosened up the dress code: the men wore suits, not tights, and Dogberry proudly paraded in Boy Scout's attire. Michael Keaton's Dogberry and Ben Elton's Verges, from Branagh's 1993 film, made a memorable entrance on pantomimed horses, a gag lifted from the movie *Monty Python and the Holy Grail* (1975).

0: Stage Direction: ***compartner:*** partner

1: "Are you good men and true?": Engraving by Byam Shaw, from 1900
By permission of the Folger Shakespeare Library

2: **salvation:** He means "damnation."

5: **any allegiance:** He means "no allegiance." Dogberry frequently uses words or phrases opposite in meaning to what he intends.

6: **charge:** orders, duties for the night

7: **most desertless:** he means "least deserving"

10: **Fortune:** It's not clear whether Dogberry believes that reading and writing are not taught, but his malapropism suggests he is in earnest.

Enter DOGBERRY and his compartner [VERGES] with the WATCH

DOGBERRY
Are you good men and true?

VERGES
Yea, or else it were pity but they should suffer salvation, body and soul.

DOGBERRY
Nay, that were a punishment too good for them, if they should have any allegiance in them, being chosen for the Prince's Watch. 5

VERGES
Well, give them their charge, neighbor Dogberry.

DOGBERRY
First, who think you the most desertless man to be Constable?

FIRST WATCHMAN
Hugh Oatcake sir, or George Seacoal, for they can write and read.

DOGBERRY
Come hither neighbor Seacoal. God hath blessed you with a good name. To be a well-favored man is the gift of Fortune, but to write 10
and read comes by Nature.

FIRST WATCHMAN
Both which Master Constable–

tracks 23-25

1-23
William Fulton as Dogberry and Roger Crowther as Verges
Bryan Pringle as Dogberry, Raymond Bowers as Verges,
Alisdair Simpson as First Watch, and Chris Pavlo as Second Watch

16: **senseless:** he means "sensible"

18: **comprehend:** he means "apprehend"; **vagrom:** he means "vagrant"

23: **knave:** rogue, rascal

24: **bidden:** bid

28: **tolerable:** he means "intolerable"

27-28: "You shall also make no noise in the streets, for, for the Watch to babble and to talk is most tolerable and not to be endured.": Jerry Stiller as Dogberry in the New York Public Theater's 1987 production directed by Gerald Freedman
Photo: George E. Joseph

30: **ancient:** old and wise

32: **bills:** weapons carried by watchmen

DOGBERRY
You have. I knew it would be your answer. Well, for your favor,
sir, why, give God thanks and make no boast of it, and for your
writing and reading, let that appear when there is no need of such   15
vanity. You are thought here to be the most senseless and fit man
for the Constable of the Watch. Therefore, bear you the lantern.
This is your charge: you shall comprehend all vagrom men; you
are to bid any man stand in the Prince's name.

SECOND WATCHMAN
How if a will not stand?   20

DOGBERRY
Why then, take no note of him, but let him go and presently call
the rest of the Watch together and thank God you are rid of a
knave.

VERGES
If he will not stand when he is bidden, he is none of the Prince's
subjects.   25

DOGBERRY
True, and they are to meddle with none but the Prince's subjects.
You shall also make no noise in the streets, for, for the Watch to
babble and to talk is most tolerable and not to be endured.

FIRST WATCHMAN
We will rather sleep than talk. We know what belongs to a Watch.

DOGBERRY
Why, you speak like an ancient and most quiet watchman, for I   30
cannot see how sleeping should offend. Only, have a care that
your bills be not stolen. Well, you are to call at all the alehouses
and bid those that are drunk get them to bed.

SECOND WATCHMAN
How if they will not?

40: **true:** honest

43-44: **they that touch pitch...defiled:** (proverbial); **pitch:** black tar, emblematic of moral depravity. See *Othello*: "So will I turn her virtue into pitch" (2.3).

Martin Spencer as Hugh Oatcake, Todd Sandomirsky as Robert Armin, John Stead as William Kemp, Michael Halberstam as Richard Cowley, Wayne Best as George Seacoal, Brian Tree as Verges, and Brian Bedford as Dogberry in the Stratford Festival of Canada's 1991 production directed by Richard Monette

Photo: Tom Skudra; Courtesy: Stratford Festival of Canada Archives

54-55: **for the ewe... calf when he bleats:** more linguistic entanglements: lambs bleat, calves neither bleat nor bay

DOGBERRY

Why then, let them alone till they are sober. If they make you not,   35
then the better answer; you may say they are not the men you
took them for.

SECOND WATCHMAN

Well, sir.

DOGBERRY

If you meet a thief, you may suspect him by virtue of your office
to be no true man, and, for such kind of men, the less you meddle   40
or make with them, why the more is for your honesty.

SECOND WATCHMAN

If we know him to be a thief, shall we not lay hands on him?

DOGBERRY

Truly, by your office you may, but I think they that touch pitch
will be defiled. The most peaceable way for you, if you do take a
thief, is to let him show himself what he is and steal out of your   45
company.

VERGES

You have been always called a merciful man, partner.

DOGBERRY

Truly, I would not hang a dog, by my will, much more a man who
hath any honesty in him.

VERGES

If you hear a child cry in the night you must call to the nurse and   50
bid her still it.

SECOND WATCHMAN

How if the nurse be asleep and will not hear us?

DOGBERRY

Why then, depart in peace, and let the child wake her with crying,
for the ewe that will not hear her lamb when it bays will never
answer a calf when he bleats.   55

57-59: "You, Constable, are to present the Prince's own person. If you meet the Prince in the night, you may stay him.": Richard Ziman as Dogberry, Edwin C. Owens as Verges, and Edward Placer, Joe Tapper, and Matthew Pendergast as members of the ensemble in the Shakespeare Theatre Company's 2002-2003 production directed by Mark Lamos

Photo: Carol Rosegg

59: **stay:** stop

60: **birlady:** short for "By your lady," an oath

61: **statues:** He means "statutes." The quarto actually prints "statutes," but, given Dogberry's propensity to garble language, the folio reading is just as appropriate.

67: **weight:** weighty or important; **coil:** turmoil, as in *Titus Andronicus*: "And wilt thou have a reason for these coils?" (3.1)

73: **coil:** turmoil, as in *Titus Andronicus*: "And wilt thou have a reason for these coils?" (3.1); **vigitant:** He means "vigilant."

73: Stage Direction: ***BORACHIO:*** Spanish word for drunkard

VERGES
    'Tis very true.

DOGBERRY
    This is the end of the charge. You, Constable, are to present the
    Prince's own person. If you meet the Prince in the night, you may
    stay him.

VERGES
    Nay, birlady, that I think a cannot.   60

DOGBERRY
    Five shillings to one on't with any man that knows the statues, he
    may stay him, marry, not without the Prince be willing, for indeed
    the Watch ought to offend no man, and it is an offense to stay a
    man against his will.

VERGES
    Birlady, I think it be so.   65

DOGBERRY
    Ha, ah ha, well, masters, good night, and there be any matter of
    weight chances, call up me. Keep your fellow's counsels and your
    own and good night. Come neighbor.

                                                                    [Going]

FIRST WATCHMAN
    Well, masters, we hear our charge. Let us go sit here upon the
    church bench till two, and then all to bed.   70

DOGBERRY
    One word more, honest neighbors. I pray you, watch about Signor
    Leonato's door, for the wedding being there tomorrow, there is a
    great coil tonight. Adieu. Be vigitant, I beseech you.

                            Exeunt [DOGBERRY and VERGES]
                            Enter BORACHIO and CONRAD

BORACHIO
    What, Conrad?

78: **Mass:** "By the mass," an oath; **my elbow itched...scab follow:** Borachio suggests that Conrad is a kind of parasite.

80: **penthouse:** awning

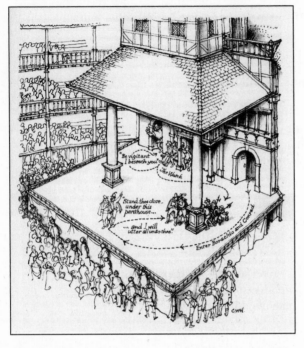

Staging of a "penthouse" under which Borachio and Conrad stand shortly before their capture

Drawing by C. Walter Hodges by permission of Cambridge University Press

82: **treason:** treachery

89: **unconfirmed:** inexperience; **fashion:** particular style or design. Shakespeare also rails against fashion in *Taming of the Shrew* (4.3).

FIRST WATCHMAN
    Peace, stir not.   75

BORACHIO
    Conrad, I say.

CONRAD
    Here man, I am at thy elbow.

BORACHIO
    Mass, and my elbow itched; I thought there would a scab follow.

CONRAD
    I will owe thee an answer for that, and now forward with thy tale.

BORACHIO
    Stand thee close then under this penthouse, for it drizzles rain,   80
    and I will, like a true drunkard, utter all to thee.

FIRST WATCHMAN
    Some treason, masters, yet stand close.

BORACHIO
    Therefore know, I have earned of Don John a thousand ducats.

CONRAD
    Is it possible that any villainy should be so dear?

BORACHIO
    Thou shouldst rather ask if it were possible any villainy should be   85
    so rich? For when rich villains have need of poor ones, poor ones
    may make what price they will.

CONRAD
    I wonder at it.

BORACHIO
    That shows thou art unconfirmed. Thou knowest that the fashion
    of a doublet or a hat or a cloak is nothing to a man.   90

92: **the fashion:** the design or cut

93: **is the fashion:** is in style

100: **vane:** weather vane

102: **hot-bloods:** i.e., hot-blooded men

103: **fashioning them:** making them appear; **Pharaoh's soldiers:** (biblical) "Pharaoh" was the title of the ancient king of Egypt under whom the Exodus of the Israelites took place.

104: **reechy:** smoky, squalid; **Bel's priests:** priests killed for the worship of false gods

105: **Hercules:** confused with Samson, who lost his strength when his wife cut his hair

106: **codpiece:** a fashionable jock strap worn on top of pants

107: **massy:** massive

CONRAD
  Yes, it is apparel.

BORACHIO
  I mean the fashion.

CONRAD
  Yes, the fashion is the fashion.

BORACHIO
  Tush, I may as well say the fool's the fool, but seest thou not what
  a deformed thief this fashion is?   95

SECOND WATCHMAN
  [Whispering] I know that Deformed. A has been a vile thief this
  seven year; a goes up and down like a gentleman. I remember his
  name.

BORACHIO
  Didst thou not hear somebody?

CONRAD
  No, 'twas the vane on the house.   100

BORACHIO
  Seest thou not, I say, what a deformed thief this fashion is, how
  giddily a turns about all the hot-bloods between fourteen and five
  and thirty, sometimes fashioning them like Pharaoh's soldiers in
  the reechy painting, sometime like god Bel's priests in the old
  Church window, sometime like the shaven Hercules in the   105
  smirched worm-eaten tapestry, where his codpiece seems as
  massy as his club?

CONRAD
  All this I see, and I see that the fashion wears out more apparel
  than the man. But art not thou thyself giddy with the fashion too
  that thou hast shifted out of thy tale into telling me of the fashion?   110

tracks 26-28

111-139
Don Meyers as Conrad and Edwin Rubin as Borachio
Alan Ayckbourn as Conrad and Peter Birrel as Borachio

111-112: "Not so neither, but know that I have tonight wooed Margaret, the Lady Hero's gentlewoman, by the name of Hero.": Michael Polak as Borachio and Michael Tisdale as Conrad in the Shakespeare Theatre Company's 2002-2003 production directed by Mark Lamos

Photo: Carol Rosegg

114: **vilely:** badly

115: **possessed:** given false information

116: **amiable:** amorous

121: **possessed:** perhaps a reference to demonic possession

128: **recovered:** he means "uncovered" or "discovered"

129: **lechery:** he means "treachery"

131: **Deformed:** The Watchman thinks that there is an accomplice named "Deformed."

131: **lock:** a lock of hair, stylishly curled

133: **made:** rewarded

BORACHIO

Not so neither, but know that I have tonight wooed Margaret, the
Lady Hero's gentlewoman, by the name of Hero. She leans me out
at her mistress' chamber-window, bids me a thousand times good
night. I tell this tale vilely. I should first tell thee how the Prince,
Claudio, and my master, planted and placed and possessed by my   115
master Don John, saw afar off in the orchard this amiable
encounter—

CONRAD

And thought they Margaret was Hero?

BORACHIO

Two of them did, the Prince and Claudio, but the devil, my master, knew she was Margaret and partly by his oaths, which first   120
possessed them, partly by the dark night, which did deceive them,
but chiefly, by my villainy, which did confirm any slander that
Don John had made. Away went Claudio enraged, swore he
would meet her as he was appointed next morning at the temple,
and there, before the whole congregation, shame her with what he   125
saw o'ernight and send her home again without a husband.

SECOND WATCHMAN *[Coming forward]*

We charge you in the Prince's name, stand.

FIRST WATCHMAN

Call up the right Master Constable. We have here recovered the
most dangerous piece of lechery that ever was known in the
commonwealth.   130

SECOND WATCHMAN

And one Deformed is one of them, I know him. A wears a lock.

CONRAD

Masters, masters.

FIRST WATCHMAN

[To SECOND WATCHMAN] You'll be made. Bring Deformed
forth I warrant you.

tracks 26-28

111-139
Don Meyers as Conrad and Edwin Rubin as Borachio
Alan Ayckbourn as Conrad and Peter Birrel as Borachio

135: **SECOND WATCHMAN: Masters, never speak:** Assigned to Conrad in the folio, but as Theobald (1733) points out, "It is evident that Conrade is...interrupted...by the impertinence of the men in office."

136: **obey you:** i.e., make you obey us

137: **commodity:** a rich prize

138: **bills:** 1) weapons used by watchmen, and 2) "bills of goods" or invoices

139: **in question:** likely to be investigated at a trial

SECOND WATCHMAN

   [To BORACHIO and CONRAD] Masters, never speak. We charge   135
you, let us obey you to go with us.

BORACHIO

   We are like to prove a goodly commodity, being taken up of these
men's bills.

CONRAD

   A commodity in question I warrant you. Come, we'll obey you.

                                             Exeunt

4: **Well:** very well

5: **rebato:** collar of some sort for her dress

6: "No pray thee, good Meg, I'll wear this.": Rachel Kempson as Ursula, Geraldine McEwan as Hero, and Zoe Caldwell as Margaret in the 1958 RSC production directed by Douglas Seale

Photo: Angus McBean © Royal Shakespeare Company

7: **troth:** truth's honor

9: **'tire:** attire

12: **exceeds:** surpasses

Act 3, Scene 4]

Enter HERO, and MARGARET, and URSULA

HERO
Good Ursula, wake my cousin Beatrice and desire her to rise.

URSULA
I will, lady.

HERO
And bid her come hither.

URSULA
Well.

MARGARET
Troth, I think your other rebato were better.   5

HERO
No pray thee, good Meg, I'll wear this.

MARGARET
By my troth, 's not so good, and I warrant your cousin will say so.

HERO
My cousin's a fool, and thou art another. I'll wear none but this.

MARGARET
I like the new 'tire within excellently, if the hair were a thought
browner. And your gown's a most rare fashion, i'faith. I saw the   10
Duchess of Milan's gown that they praise so.

HERO
O that exceeds, they say.

14: **down sleeves:** long, close-fitting sleeves

14-15: **side sleeves:** long sleeves hanging from the shoulder

15: **underborne:** held up

16: **quaint:** elegant

18: **'Twill be...of a man:** i.e., she'll weigh more when she has a man lying on top of her

21: **in a beggar:** i.e., even in a beggar

22: **Saving your reverence:** phrase of apology

23: **wrest:** misinterpret

29: **in the sick tune:** as though you were sick

MARGARET
By my troth, 's but a nightgown in respect of yours: cloth o' gold
and cuts, and laced with silver, set with pearls, down sleeves, side
sleeves, and skirts, round underborne with a bluish tinsel, but for a   15
fine, quaint, graceful, and excellent fashion, yours is worth ten on't.

HERO
God give me joy to wear it, for my heart is exceeding heavy.

MARGARET
'Twill be heavier soon—by the weight of a man.

HERO
Fie upon thee, art not ashamed?

MARGARET
Of what, lady? Of speaking honorably? Is not marriage honorable   20
in a beggar? Is not your lord honorable without marriage? I think
you would have me say, "Saving your reverence, a husband." An
bad thinking do not wrest true speaking, I'll offend nobody. Is
there any harm in thee heavier for a husband? None, I think, an
it be the right husband and the right wife, otherwise 'tis light and   25
not heavy. Ask my Lady Beatrice else. Here she comes.

                                          Enter BEATRICE

HERO
Good morrow, coz.

BEATRICE
Good morrow, sweet Hero.

HERO
Why, how now? Do you speak in the sick tune?

BEATRICE
I am out of all other tune, methinks.   30

27-68
Faith Ward as Hero, Maureen Fitzgerald as Beatrice,
and Flora Montgomery as Margaret
Abigail Docherty as Hero, Saskia Reeves as Beatrice,
and Amanda Root as Margaret

31: **'s:** us; **Light o' Love:** an old dance tune

31-33: **Clap 's into...with your heels:** a bawdy joke. "Burden" refers to the weight of a man (3.4.18) and "light-heeled" means promiscuous.

33-34: **Then if your husband...lack no barns:** Beatrice continues the bawdy exchange. "Barns" is a pun on "bairns," meaning children.

35: **illegitimate construction:** a pun, referring to the children (bastards) conceived in the barn

37: **heigh-ho:** echoes Beatrice's speech at 2.1.243: "Heigh-ho for a husband"

40: **turned Turk:** turned faithless or renounced one's faith. Perhaps the joke here is that if she "turned Turk" she would not know which wants more, a hawk, horse, or husband.

42: **trow:** I wonder

46: **A maid...catching of cold:** more bawdiness. Margaret suggests that Beatrice is, or wants to be, stuffed with a man or perhaps pregnant.

MARGARET

Clap 's into "Light o' Love", that goes without a burden. Do you
sing it, and I'll dance it.

BEATRICE

Ye "Light o' Love" with your heels. Then if your husband have
stables enough, you'll see he shall lack no barns.

MARGARET

O illegitimate construction! I scorn that with my heels.   35

BEATRICE

'Tis almost five o'clock, cousin. 'Tis time you were ready. By my
troth, I am exceeding ill, heigh-ho.

MARGARET

For a hawk, a horse, or a husband?

BEATRICE

For the letter that begins them all, H.

MARGARET

Well, an you be not turned Turk, there's no more sailing by the   40
star.

BEATRICE

What means the fool, trow?

MARGARET

Nothing I, but God send everyone their heart's desire.

HERO

These gloves the Count sent me, they are an excellent perfume.

BEATRICE

I am stuffed, cousin. I cannot smell.   45

MARGARET

A maid and stuffed! There's goodly catching of cold.

tracks 29-31

27-68
Faith Ward as Hero, Maureen Fitzgerald as Beatrice,
and Flora Montgomery as Margaret
Abigail Docherty as Hero, Saskia Reeves as Beatrice,
and Amanda Root as Margaret

51: **sick:** Margaret takes this to mean "sick in love" and that Beatrice is suffering from the *Benedick* or *benedictus*. See 1.1.63-66, where Beatrice suggests that Benedick is a disease.

52: *carduus benedictus:* the herb "holy thistle," which is a salve (*carduus* = thistle; *benedictus* = holy, and also a pun on "Benedick")

53: **qualm:** cold

55: **moral:** meaning

BEATRICE

O God help me, God help me, how long have you professed
apprehension?

MARGARET

Ever since you left it. Doth not my wit become me rarely?

BEATRICE

It is not seen enough. You should wear it in your cap. By my troth,   50
I am sick.

MARGARET

Get you some of this distilled *carduus benedictus* and lay it to
your heart. It is the only thing for a qualm.

HERO

There thou prick'st her with a thistle.

BEATRICE

Benedictus, why *benedictus*? You have some moral in this   55
benedictus?

MARGARET

Moral? No, by my troth, I have no moral meaning. I meant plain
holy thistle. You may think perchance that I think you are in
love–Nay, birlady, I am not such a fool to think what I list, nor I
list not to think what I can, nor indeed, I cannot think if I would   60
think my heart out of thinking that you are in love, or that you
will be in love, or that you can be in love. Yet Benedick was such
another, and now is he become a man. He swore he would never
marry, and yet now, in despite of his heart, he eats his meat
without grudging. And how you may be converted I know not,   65
but methinks you look with your eyes as other women do.

BEATRICE

What pace is this that thy tongue keeps?

tracks 29-31

27-68
Faith Ward as Hero, Maureen Fitzgerald as Beatrice,
and Flora Montgomery as Margaret
Abigail Docherty as Hero, Saskia Reeves as Beatrice,
and Amanda Root as Margaret

68: **Not a false gallop:** She might speak as fast as a horse gallops, but what she says is not false.

MARGARET
  Not a false gallop.

Enter URSULA

URSULA
  Madam, withdraw. The Prince, the Count, Signor Benedick, Don
  John, and all the gallants of the town are come to fetch you to   70
  church.

HERO
  Help me to dress me good coz, good Meg, good Ursula–

[Exeunt]

2: **confidence:** he means "conference;" **decerns:** he means "concerns"

9: **blunt:** he means "sharp"

10: Scene: **the skin between his brows:** In the early nineteenth century, Robert Kee-ley was applauded for his Verges, especially his acting on this line. Walter Goodman records that "when his [Keeley's] asinine chief patted him on the head, and he at first bent under the honour, and then became the taller for it, gazing into his patron's face with an expression of fatuous contentment perfectly marvelous."

13: **odorous:** he means "odious;" **palabras:** Steevens (1773) suggests that this means "few words" ("palabras" is the Spanish for "words") after Sly's use in *Taming of the Shrew* (1.5). However, Dogberry could also mean "parable" or "stories," as in "comparing stories is odious."

Act 3, Scene 5]

Enter LEONATO, [DOGBERRY] and
[VERGES] the HEADBOROUGH

LEONATO
What would you with me, honest neighbor?

DOGBERRY
Marry, sir, I would have some confidence with you that decerns
you nearly.

LEONATO
Brief, I pray you, for you see it is a busy time with me.

DOGBERRY
Marry, this it is, sir.   5

[VERGES]
Yes, in truth, it is, sir.

LEONATO
What is it, my good friends?

DOGBERRY
Goodman Verges, sir, speaks a little off the matter. An old man,
sir, and his wits are not so blunt, as, God help, I would desire they
were, but, in faith, honest as the skin between his brows.   10

[VERGES]
Yes, I thank God, I am as honest as any man living that is an old
man, and no honester than I.

DOGBERRY
Comparisons are odorous palabras, neighbor Verges.

14: **tedious:** He confuses "tedious" with some compliment, possibly "virtuous."

15-16: **poor Duke's officers:** he means "Duke's poor officers"

20: **exclamation:** he means "acclamation"

24: **tonight:** last night; **expecting:** respecting

26-27: **When the age is in, the wit is out:** The proverb is actually "When the ale is in, the wit is out."

32: **he comes too short of you:** i.e., he's not as grand as you are; probably meant as a backhanded compliment

LEONATO
Neighbors, you are tedious.

DOGBERRY
It pleases your worship to say so, but we are the poor Duke's   15
officers. But truly, for mine own part, if I were as tedious as a
king, I could find in my heart to bestow it all of your worship.

LEONATO
All thy tediousness on me, ah?

DOGBERRY
Yea, and 'twere a thousand pound more than 'tis, for I hear as
good exclamation on your worship as of any man in the city, and,   20
though I be but a poor man, I am glad to hear it.

[VERGES]
And so am I.

LEONATO
I would fain know what you have to say.

[VERGES]
Marry sir, our Watch tonight, excepting your worship's presence,
ha' ta'en a couple of as arrant knaves as any in Messina.   25

DOGBERRY
A good old man sir; he will be talking. As they say, "When the age
is in, the wit is out." God help us, it is a world to see. Well said,
i'faith, neighbor Verges. Well, God's a good man, and two men
ride of a horse, one must ride behind. An honest soul, i'faith sir, by
my troth, he is, as ever broke bread. But God is to be worshipped.   30
All men are not alike, alas good neighbor.

LEONATO
Indeed, neighbor, he comes too short of you.

DOGBERRY
Gifts that God gives.

35: **comprehended:** he means "apprehended"

36: **aspicious:** he means "suspicious"

40: **suffigance:** he means "sufficient"

45: **gaol:** jail; **examination:** he means "examine"

49: **noncome:** he means "nonplus" (perplexed)

50: **excommunication**: he means "examination"

LEONATO
I must leave you.

[Going]

DOGBERRY
One word sir. Our Watch, sir, have indeed comprehended two   35
aspicious persons, and we would have them this morning
examined before your worship.

LEONATO
Take their examination yourself and bring it me. I am now in
great haste, as it may appear unto you.

DOGBERRY
It shall be suffigance.   40

LEONATO
Drink some wine ere you go, fare you well.

[Enter MESSENGER]

MESSENGER
My lord, they stay for you to give your daughter to her husband.

LEONATO
I'll wait upon them. I am ready.

[Exeunt LEONATO and MESSENGER]

DOGBERRY
Go, good partner, go get you to Francis Seacoal. Bid him bring his
pen and inkhorn to the gaol. We are now to examination these   45
men.

VERGES
And we must do it wisely.

DOGBERRY
We will spare for no wit, I warrant you. *[Pointing to his head]*
Here's that shall drive some of them to a noncome. Only get the
learned writer to set down our excommunication, and meet me at   50
the jail.

Exeunt

[Much Ado About Nothing

Nothing

Act 4

0: Scene: Henry Irving's 1882 Lyceum production featured an Italian cathedral with stained-glass windows and statues of saints, thirty-foot-high pillars, a canopied roof of crimson plush from which hung golden lamps, a floor covered with vases of flowers, and flaming candles rising to a height of eighteen feet. The set for Edward Gordon Craig's 1903-04 production relied more on nuances of lighting. For the church scene, Craig cast a pool of light on the floor that appeared to have been filtered through a stained-glass window.

6: "Lady, you come hither to be married to this Count?": Kathleen Early as Hero, Edwin C. Owens as Friar Francis, and Barrett Foa as Claudio in the Shakespeare Theatre Company's 2002-2003 production directed by Mark Lamos
Photo: Carol Rosegg

8: **inward:** private, yet undisclosed

Act 4, Scene 1]

Enter DON PEDRO, JOHN THE BASTARD,
LEONATO, FRIAR, CLAUDIO, BENEDICK,
HERO, and BEATRICE

LEONATO
Come, Friar Francis, be brief. Only to the plain form of marriage,
and you shall recount their particular duties afterwards.

FRIAR
You come hither, my lord, to marry this lady?

CLAUDIO
No.

LEONATO
To be married to her, Friar. You come to marry her.   5

FRIAR
Lady, you come hither to be married to this Count?

HERO
I do.

FRIAR
If either of you know any inward impediment why you should not
be conjoined, I charge you on your souls to utter it.

CLAUDIO
Know you any, Hero?   10

HERO
None my lord.

FRIAR
Know you any, Count?

23: **counterpoise:** equal in weight or fortune

25: **learn me:** teach me

27: **rotten orange:** rotten to the core, playing on the earlier pun on civil and orange (2.1.224)

28: **She's but...of honor:** she only *appears* honest and honorable

36: **the heat of a luxurious bed:** the passion of lovemaking; see *Hamlet*: "[lust], though to a radiant angel link'd / Will sate itself in a celestial bed / And prey on garbage" (1.5)

37: "Her blush is guiltiness, not modesty.": John Franklyn-Robbins as Don Pedro, Peter Dvorsky as Benedick, John Neville as Leonato, Maria Ricossa as Margaret, Shelagh McLeod as Ursula, Tana Hicken as Beatrice, Diana Fajrajsi as Hero, Daniel Libman as Friar Francis, and Colm Feore as Claudio in the Stratford Festival of Canada's 1983 production directed by Michael Langham
Photo: Robert C. Ragsdale; Courtesy: Stratford Festival of Canada Archives

LEONATO

I dare make his answer: none.

CLAUDIO

O what men dare do! What men may do! What men daily do, not
knowing what they do!   15

BENEDICK

How now! Interjections? Why then, some be of laughing, as "ah,
ha, he."

CLAUDIO

Stand thee by, Friar. *[To LEONATO]* Father, by your leave,
Will you with free and unconstrained soul give
Me this maid, your daughter?   20

LEONATO

As freely, son, as God did give her me.

CLAUDIO

And what have I to give you back, whose worth
May counterpoise this rich and precious gift?

DON PEDRO

Nothing, unless you render her again.

CLAUDIO

Sweet Prince, you learn me noble thankfulness.   25
There Leonato, take her back again.
Give not this rotten orange to your friend.
She's but the sign and semblance of her honor.
Behold how like a maid she blushes here!
O what authority and show of truth   30
Can cunning sin cover itself withal!
Comes not that blood as modest evidence
To witness simple virtue? Would you not swear,
All you that see her, that she were a maid
By these exterior shows? But she is none.   35
She knows the heat of a luxurious bed.
Her blush is guiltiness, not modesty.

39: **approved wanton:** known whore

40–42: **if you...defeat of her virginity:** if you have overcome her resistance and slept with her already

43: **known her:** i.e., had sexual relations with her

45: **forehand sin:** i.e., the sin of having sexual relations before marriage (forehand = beforehand)

46: **too large:** improper

48: **comely:** proper

57: "Sweet Prince, why speak not you?": Elizabeth Waterston as Hero and Sam Waterston as Leonato in The Public Theater 2004 production directed by David Esbjornson
Photo: Michal Daniel

51: **Dian:** Goddess of Chastity

53: **blood:** sexual desire

54: **Venus:** Goddess of Love

56: **so wide:** oddly, crazily

LEONATO
    What do you mean, my lord?

CLAUDIO
                    Not to be married,
    Not to knit my soul to an approved wanton.

LEONATO
    Dear my lord, if you in your own proof   40
    Have vanquished the resistance of her youth
    And made defeat of her virginity—

CLAUDIO
    I know what you would say. If I have known her,
    You will say, she did embrace me as a husband,
    And so extenuate the forehand sin. No, Leonato,   45
    I never tempted her with word too large
    But, as a brother to his sister, showed
    Bashful sincerity and comely love.

HERO
    And seemed I ever otherwise to you?

CLAUDIO
    Out on thy seeming! I will write against it.   50
    You seem to me as Dian in her orb,
    As chaste as is the bud ere it be blown.
    But you are more intemperate in your blood
    Than Venus or those pampered animals
    That rage in savage sensuality.   55

HERO
    Is my lord well that he doth speak so wide?

LEONATO
    Sweet Prince, why speak not you?

59: **a common stale:** a common whore

66: "All this is so, but what of this my lord?": Robert O'Mahoney as Claudio, Edward Jewesbury as Leonato, and Joanna Foster as Hero in the 1982 RSC production directed by Terry Hands
Photo: Donald Cooper

67: **move:** ask

68: **fatherly and kindly power:** paternal authority

DON PEDRO
                    What should I speak?
I stand dishonored that have gone about
To link my dear friend to a common stale.

LEONATO
Are these things spoken, or do I but dream?   60

JOHN
Sir, they are spoken, and these things are true.

BENEDICK
This looks not like a nuptial.

HERO
                    True! O God!

CLAUDIO
Leonato, stand I here?
Is this the Prince? Is this the Prince's brother?
Is this face Hero's? Are our eyes our own?   65

LEONATO
All this is so, but what of this my lord?

CLAUDIO
Let me but move one question to your daughter,
And, by that fatherly and kindly power
That you have in her, bid her answer truly.

LEONATO
I charge thee do so, as thou art my child.   70

HERO
O God defend me! How am I beset!
What kind of catechizing call you this?

CLAUDIO
To make you answer truly to your name.

74: **blot:** erase

76-77: "What man was he talked with you yesternight / Out at your window betwixt twelve and one?": Malcolm Armstrong as Friar Francis, Leon Pownall as Claudio, Pamela Brook as Hero, William Needles as Leonato, and Powys Thomas as Antonio in the Stratford Festival of Canada's 1971 production directed by William Hutt
Photo: Douglas Spillane; Courtesy: Stratford Festival of Canada Archives

86: **liberal:** frank, free

87–88: **vile encounters... A thousand times:** See *Othello*: "She was false as water..../ Cassio did top her; ask thy husband.../Thy husband knew all" (5.2).

93: **misgovernment:** bad behavior. See *The Rape of Lucrece*: "Black lust, dishonor, shame, misgoverning..." (654).

100: **conjecture:** suspicion

102: **gracious:** attractive

HERO
    Is it not Hero? Who can blot that name
    With any just reproach?

CLAUDIO
                  Marry, that can Hero.   75
    Hero itself can blot out Hero's virtue.
    What man was he talked with you yesternight
    Out at your window betwixt twelve and one?
    Now, if you are a maid, answer to this.

HERO
    I talked with no man at that hour, my lord.   80

DON PEDRO
    Why then are you no maiden. Leonato,
    I am sorry you must hear. Upon mine honor,
    Myself, my brother, and this grievèd Count
    Did see her, hear her at that hour last night
    Talk with a ruffian at her chamber window,   85
    Who hath, indeed, most like a liberal villain,
    Confessed the vile encounters they have had
    A thousand times in secret.

JOHN
    Fie, fie, they are not to be named my lord,
    Not to be spoke of.   90
    There is not chastity enough in language
    Without offense to utter them. Thus, pretty lady,
    I am sorry for thy much misgovernment.

CLAUDIO
    O Hero! What a Hero hadst thou been
    If half thy outward graces had been placed   95
    About thy thoughts and counsels of thy heart.
    But fare thee well, most foul, most fair, farewell,
    Thou pure impiety and impious purity,
    For thee I'll lock up all the gates of love,
    And on my eyelids shall conjecture hang   100
    To turn all beauty into thoughts of harm,
    And never shall it more be gracious.

104: **wherefore:** why

106: **Smother her spirits up:** let her die

108: "Hero, why Hero, uncle, Signor Benedick, Friar": Engraving by Byam Shaw, from 1900

By permission of the Folger Shakespeare Library

109: **Fate:** the Goddess of Destiny

LEONATO
Hath no man's dagger here a point for me?

[HERO faints]

BEATRICE
Why, how now cousin, wherefore sink you down?

JOHN
Come, let us go. These things come thus to light   105
Smother her spirits up.

BENEDICK
How doth the lady?

BEATRICE
                    Dead I think! Help uncle!
Hero, why Hero, uncle, Signor Benedick, Friar.

LEONATO
O Fate! Take not away thy heavy hand.
Death is the fairest cover for her shame   110
That may be wished for.

[She revives]

BEATRICE
                    How now, cousin Hero?

FRIAR
Have comfort, lady.

LEONATO
                    Dost thou look up?

FRIAR
Yea, wherefore should she not?

117–119: **do not ope thy eyes... spirits stronger than thy shames:** See *Titus Androni-cus*: "Die, die, Livinia, and thy shame with thee" (5.3).

120: **on the rearward of reproaches:** i.e., after you have been reproached

122: **Chid:** complained

123: **Why had I one:** Leonato is remembering that he rued having only one child.

127: **'smirched:** besmirched, fouled; the folio prints *smeered*; **mired:** tainted

134-135: **pit of ink that the wide sea...clean again:** See *Macbeth*: "Will all great Neptune's ocean wash this blood/ Clean from my hand?" (2.2).

137: **tainted flesh:** unclean, corrupted body

140: **belied:** the victim of lies

LEONATO

    Wherefore? Why doth not every earthly thing
    Cry shame upon her? Could she here deny   115
    The story that is printed in her blood?
    Do not live, Hero, do not ope thine eyes;
    For did I think thou wouldst not quickly die,
    Thought I thy spirits were stronger then thy shames,
    Myself would on the rearward of reproaches   120
    Strike at thy life. Grieved I I had but one?
    Chid I for that at frugal Nature's frame?
    O, one too much by thee—Why had I one?
    Why ever wast thou lovely in my eyes?
    Why had I not with charitable hand   125
    Took up a beggar's issue at my gates
    Who, smirched thus and mired with infamy,
    I might have said, no part of it is mine.
    This shame derives itself from unknown loins,
    But mine, and mine I loved, and mine I praised,   130
    And mine that I was proud; on mine so much
    That I myself was to myself not mine,
    Valuing of her—Why she—O, she is fallen
    Into a pit of ink that the wide sea
    Hath drops too few to wash her clean again,   135
    And salt too little, which may season give
    To her foul, tainted flesh.

BENEDICK

               Sir, sir, be patient.
    For my part, I am so attired in wonder
    I know not what to say.

BEATRICE

    O, on my soul, my cousin is belied.   140

BENEDICK

    Lady, were you her bedfellow last night?

BEATRICE

    No, truly, not; although until last night,
    I have this twelvemonth been her bedfellow.

149–152: Hear me a little, for I have only been silent...apparitions: The quarto and folio set these lines in prose, but the rest of the Friar's speech is in verse. Most editors set the lines in verse, although the exact lineation differs.

152: apparitions: signs

159: experimental seal: i.e., authority based on my life experience; **warrant:** guarantee

160: The tenure of my book: my learning and logic

163: biting: grievous, mortifying

166: perjury: lying

169: "Lady, what man is he you are accused of?": Eileen Herlie as Beatrice, Diana Maddox as Hero, Mervyn Blake as Leonato, Powys Thomas as Friar Francis, and Christopher Plummer as Benedick in the Stratford Festival of Canada's 1958 production directed by Michael Langham

Photo: Herb Nott & Co. Ltd.; Courtesy: Stratford Festival of Canada Archives

LEONATO

 Confirmed, confirmed. O, that is stronger made
 Which was before barred up with ribs of iron.   145
 Would the two Princes lie, and Claudio lie,
 Who loved her so, that, speaking of her foulness,
 Washed it with tears? Hence from her, let her die.

FRIAR

 Hear me a little, for I have only been silent
 So long and given way unto this course   150
 Of fortune by noting of the lady.
 I have marked a thous'nd blushing apparitions
 To start into her face, a thousand innocent shames,
 In angel whiteness beat away those blushes,
 And in her eye there hath appeared a fire   155
 To burn the errors that these Princes hold
 Against her maiden truth. Call me a fool,
 Trust not my reading, nor my observations,
 Which with experimental seal doth warrant
 The tenure of my book; trust not my age,   160
 My reverence, calling, nor divinity,
 If this sweet lady lie not guiltless here,
 Under some biting error.

LEONATO

      Friar, it cannot be.
 Thou seest that all the grace that she hath left
 Is that she will not add to her damnation   165
 A sin of perjury. She not denies it.
 Why seek'st thou then to cover with excuse,
 That which appears in proper nakedness?

FRIAR

 Lady, what man is he you are accused of?

HERO

 They know that do accuse me; I know none.   170
 If I know more of any man alive
 Than that which maiden modesty doth warrant,

175: **unmeet:** inappropriate, improper

176: **Maintained the change of words:** i.e., conversed

178: **misprision:** misunderstanding

179: **the very bent of honor:** i.e., the quality or inclination to be honorable

181: **practice:** manipulation, plotting

182: **in frame of villainies:** for the purpose of causing mischief

189: **'reft:** left me bereft

191: **policy:** sharpness

193: **To quit me of them:** to even the score with them; **throughly:** thoroughly

198: **ostentation:** show, appearance

200: **epitaphs:** traditional poems read by friends at the grave of the departed

Let all my sins lack mercy. O, my father,
Prove you that any man with me conversed,
At hours unmeet, or that I yesternight   175
Maintained the change of words with any creature,
Refuse me, hate me, torture me to death.

FRIAR
There is some strange misprision in the Princes.

BENEDICK
Two of them have the very bent of honor,
And if their wisdoms be misled in this   180
The practice of it lives in John the Bastard,
Whose spirits toil in frame of villainies.

LEONATO
I know not. If they speak but truth of her,
These hands shall tear her. If they wrong her honor,
The proudest of them shall well hear of it.   185
Time hath not yet so dried this blood of mine,
Nor age so eat up my invention,
Nor Fortune made such havoc of my means,
Nor my bad life 'reft me so much of friends,
But they shall find, awaked in such a kind,   190
Both strength of limb and policy of mind,
Ability in means and choice of friends,
To quit me of them throughly.

FRIAR
                    Pause awhile,
And let my counsel sway you in this case.
Your daughter here the Princes left for dead.   195
Let her awhile be secretly kept in,
And publish it that she is dead indeed.
Maintain a mourning ostentation,
And on your family's old monument,
Hang mournful epitaphs, and do all rites   200
That appertain unto a burial.

206: **travail:** troubles

213: **rack the value:** overvalue

218: **study of imagination:** reflection or reveries

224: **liver:** The liver was thought to be the seat of love.

227: **success:** (of this plan)

230: **But if all aim...levelled false:** if the plan to vindicate Hero should prove unsuccessful

232: **quench the wonder of her infamy:** quiet the talk over her supposed crime

233: **sort:** turns out

LEONATO

    What shall become of this? What will this do?

FRIAR

    Marry, this well carried shall on her behalf
    Change slander to remorse. That is some good.
    But not for that dream I on this strange course, 205
    But on this travail look for greater birth.
    She dying, as it must be so maintained,
    Upon the instant that she was accused
    Shall be lamented, pitied, and excused
    Of every hearer, for it so falls out 210
    That what we have we prize not to the worth
    Whiles we enjoy it, but, being lacked and lost,
    Why then we rack the value. Then we find
    The virtue that possession would not show us
    Whiles it was ours. So will it fare with Claudio. 215
    When he shall hear she died upon his words,
    Th' idea of her life shall sweetly creep
    Into his study of imagination,
    And every lovely organ of her life
    Shall come apparelled in more precious habit, 220
    More moving delicate and full of life
    Into the eye and prospect of his soul
    Than when she lived indeed. Then shall he mourn,
    If ever love had interest in his liver,
    And wish he had not so accused her. 225
    No, though he thought his accusation true.
    Let this be so and doubt not but success
    Will fashion the event in better shape
    Than I can lay it down in likelihood.
    But if all aim but this be levelled false, 230
    The supposition of the lady's death
    Will quench the wonder of her infamy.
    And, if it sort not well, you may conceal her,
    As best befits her wounded reputation,
    In some reclusive and religious life, 235
    Out of all eyes, tongues, minds, and injuries.

238: **inwardness:** close relationship

242: **flow in grief:** cry sad tears

243: **twine:** hope

244: **Presently:** immediately

247: **prolonged:** postponed

tracks 32-34

248-291
John Horton as Benedick and Maureen Fitzgerald as Beatrice
Samuel West as Benedick and Saskia Reeves as Beatrice

248: "Lady Beatrice, have you wept all this while?": Derek Jacobi as Benedick and Sinéad Cusack as Beatrice in the 1982 RSC production directed by Terry Hands
Photo: Donald Cooper

253: **right:** revenge

BENEDICK

Signor Leonato, let the Friar advise you,
And though you know my inwardness and love
Is very much unto the Prince and Claudio.
Yet, by mine honor, I will deal in this   240
As secretly and justly as your soul
Should with your body.

LEONATO

                    Being that I flow in grief,
The smallest twine may lead me.

FRIAR

'Tis well consented. Presently away,
For to strange sores, strangely they strain the cure.   245
Come, lady, die to live. This wedding day
Perhaps is but prolonged. Have patience and endure.

                    Exeunt all but BEATRICE and BENEDICK

BENEDICK

Lady Beatrice, have you wept all this while?

BEATRICE

Yea, and I will weep a while longer.

BENEDICK

I will not desire that.   250

BEATRICE

You have no reason. I do it freely.

BENEDICK

Surely, I do believe your fair cousin is wronged.

BEATRICE

Ah, how much might the man deserve of me that would right her!

BENEDICK

Is there any way to show such friendship?

248-291
John Horton as Benedick and Maureen Fitzgerald as Beatrice
Samuel West as Benedick and Saskia Reeves as Beatrice

255: **even:** direct

257: **office:** duty

George Alexander as Benedick from his 1898 production at the St. James's Theatre (London)
By permission of the Folger Shakespeare Library

263: **By my sword:** a mild oath

264: **Do not swear and eat it:** perhaps a pun meant to recall Beatrice's earlier claim that Benedick had taken her heart and was stuffed, presumably with love of her, but soon found means to release his affections (see 1.1.43 and 2.1.212-214)

BEATRICE
A very even way, but no such friend–   255

BENEDICK
May a man do it?

BEATRICE
It is a man's office but not yours.

BENEDICK
I do love nothing in the world so well as you. Is not that strange?

BEATRICE
As strange as the thing I know not. It were as possible for me to
say, I loved nothing so well as you. But believe me not, and yet I   260
lie not; I confess nothing, nor I deny nothing. I am sorry for my
cousin.

BENEDICK
By my sword, Beatrice, thou lovest me.

BEATRICE
Do not swear and eat it.

BENEDICK
I will swear by it that you love me, and I will make him eat it that   265
says I love not you.

BEATRICE
Will you not eat your word?

BENEDICK
With no sauce that can be devised to it. I protest I love thee.

BEATRICE
Why then, God forgive me.

BENEDICK
What offense, sweet Beatrice?   270

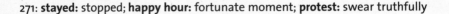

248-291
John Horton as Benedick and Maureen Fitzgerald as Beatrice
Samuel West as Benedick and Saskia Reeves as Beatrice

271: **stayed:** stopped; **happy hour:** fortunate moment; **protest:** swear truthfully

276: Scene: **Kill Claudio:** This line often gets a laugh. Gielgud and Diana Wynyard subdued "the humour of the love declaration so that Beatrice's sudden murderous entreaty [could] be received not as a climax threatening anticlimax but as a deepening of the lovers' new-found seriousness" (*Times*, 22 July 1955).

Donna Bullock as Beatrice and Sherman Howard as Benedick in The Shakespeare Theatre of New Jersey's 2003 production directed by Bonnie J. Monte
Photo: Gerry Goodstein

BEATRICE
You have stayed me in a happy hour. I was about to protest I
loved you.

BENEDICK
And do it with all thy heart.

BEATRICE
I love you with so much of my heart that none is left to protest.

BENEDICK
Come, bid me do anything for thee.   275

BEATRICE
Kill Claudio.

BENEDICK
Ha, not for the wide world.

BEATRICE
You kill me to deny it. Farewell.

[Going]

BENEDICK
Tarry, sweet Beatrice–

[Holding her]

BEATRICE
I am gone, though I am here. There is no love in you. Nay, I pray   280
you, let me go.

BENEDICK
Beatrice!

BEATRICE
In faith, I will go.

BENEDICK
We'll be friends first.

tracks 32-34

248-291
John Horton as Benedick and Maureen Fitzgerald as Beatrice
Samuel West as Benedick and Saskia Reeves as Beatrice

287: **approved:** proved to be; **height:** highest degree

289: **bear her in hand:** lead her to the Friar, as if to take vows of marriage

290: **uncovered:** publicly disclosed

291: **marketplace:** i.e., the most public place in the town

293: **A proper saying:** a likely story

297: **counties:** McEachern (2006) defines this as a "mocking term for multiple courtships;" **'count:** account

298: **Count Comfect:** Claudio seems sweet as candy but is rotten to the core. Edward Capell (1768) suggests she means *"sugar-plumed Count."*

300: **curtsies:** compliments

300-301: **But manhood is melted...into tongue:** The implication is that men are more willing to talk than fight.

301: **trim ones:** i.e., smooth talkers (trim = neat, smooth)

BEATRICE
You dare easier be friends with me than fight with mine enemy?   285

BENEDICK
Is Claudio thine enemy?

BEATRICE
Is a not approved in the height a villain that hath slandered,
scorned, dishonored my kinswoman? O that I were a man! What,
bear her in hand until they come to take hands, and then with
public accusation, uncovered slander, unmitigated rancor–O   290
God, that I were a man! I would eat his heart in the marketplace!

BENEDICK
Hear me Beatrice–

BEATRICE
Talk with a man out at a window? A proper saying–

BENEDICK
Nay, but Beatrice–

BEATRICE
Sweet Hero, she is wronged; she is slandered; she is undone.   295

BENEDICK
Beat–

BEATRICE
Princes and counties! Surely a princely testimony, a goodly 'count.
Count Comfect, a sweet gallant, surely. O that I were a man for
his sake! Or that I had any friend would be a man for my sake!
But manhood is melted into curtsies, valor into complement, and   300
men are only turned into tongue. And trim ones too! He is now as
valiant as Hercules that only tells a lie and swears it. I cannot be
a man with wishing, therefore I will die a woman with grieving.
                                        [Breaking from him. Going.]

308: "Enough, I am engaged. I will challenge him.": Josie Lawrence as Benedick and Yolanda Vazquez as Beatrice in the all-female 2004 production at the Shakespeare's Globe Theatre directed by Tamara Harvey

Photo: Donald Cooper

308: **I am engaged:** a grim pun. While declaring his love and promise of marriage (thus engagement), he also promises to engage Claudio in a duel.

309-310: **render me a dear account:** pay dearly

BENEDICK
Tarry, good Beatrice. By this hand, I love thee.

BEATRICE
Use it for my love some other way than swearing by it.   305

BENEDICK
Think you in your soul the Count Claudio hath wronged Hero?

BEATRICE
Yea, as sure as I have a thought or a soul.

BENEDICK
Enough, I am engaged. I will challenge him. I will kiss your hand.
[Kisses her hand]
And so I leave you. By this hand Claudio shall render me a dear
account. As you hear of me, so think of me. Go comfort your   310
cousin. I must say she is dead, and so farewell.
[Exeunt]

0: Stage Direction: ***gowns***: official garb of constables and the sexton

1-70: The folio assigns some lines in this scene to *"Cowley," "Andrew,"* and *"Kemp,"* actors in Shakespeare's troupe, instead of the characters they play. Following the approach of modern texts, the lines have been reassigned to the characters.

1: **dissembly:** he means "assembly"

4: **Marry...my partner**: Verges confuses "malefactors" with "officers"; perhaps he was confused by "factor," meaning an official agent.

5: **exhibition:** perhaps he means "commission"

8: "Yea marry, let them come before me. What is your name, friend?": Christopher Luscombe as Dogberry, Christopher Gee as Conrad, and Patrick Baladi as Borachio in the 1996 RSC production directed by Michael Boyd
Photo: Reg Wilson © Royal Shakespeare Company

10: **sirrah:** term of address for a male of inferior social standing

Act 4, Scene 2]

Enter DOGBERRY, [VERGES] and WATCH, BORACHIO,
and the [SEXTON] in gowns

[DOGBERRY]
Is our whole dissembly appeared?

[VERGES]
O, a stool and a cushion for the Sexton.

[SEXTON sits]

SEXTON
Which be the malefactors?

[VERGES]
Marry, that am I, and my partner.

[SECOND WATCHMAN]
Nay, that's certain. We have the exhibition to examine.   5

SEXTON
But which are the offenders that are to be examined? Let them
come before, Master Constable.

[DOGBERRY]
Yea marry, let them come before me. What is your name, friend?

BORACHIO
Borachio.

[DOGBERRY]
[To the SEXTON] Pray, write down "Borachio." Yours, sirrah?   10

CONRAD
I am a gentleman, sir, and my name is Conrad.

16: **defend but:** forbid that

21: **witty:** clever

22: **go about with him:** work on him

25: **they are both in a tale:** i.e., both agree on their stories

29: **eftest:** Dogberry means "deftest," though A.R. Humphreys (1981) suggests "aptest."

[DOGBERRY]
Write down "Master Gentleman Conrad." Masters, do you serve God?

CONRAD and BORACHIO
Yea, sir, we hope.

[DOGBERRY]
Write down that they "*hope* they serve God," and write God   15
first, for God defend but God should go before such villains.
[To CONRAD and BORACHIO] Masters, it is proved already
that you are little better than false knaves, and it will go near to
be thought so shortly. How answer you for yourselves?

CONRAD
Marry, sir, we say we are none.   20

[DOGBERRY]
[To SEXTON] A marvelous witty fellow, I assure you, but I will
go about with him. *[To BORACHIO]* Come you hither, sirrah. A
word in your ear, sir. I say to you, it is thought you are false knaves.

BORACHIO
Sir, I say to you we are none.

[DOGBERRY]
Well, stand aside. 'Fore God they are both in a tale. *[To SEXTON]*   25
Have you writ down that they are none?

SEXTON
Master Constable, you go not the way to examine. You must call
forth the Watch that are their accusers.

[DOGBERRY]
Yea, marry, that's the eftest way. Let the Watch come forth.
Masters, I charge you in the Prince's name, accuse these men.   30

FIRST WATCHMAN
This man said, sir, that Don John, the Prince's brother, was a villain.

32: **perjury:** he means "slander" or "treachery"

39: **flat burglary:** he means "bribery"

40: **by th' Mass:** mild oath; from the folio; the quarto prints "by mass"

44: **redemption:** he means "damnation"

[DOGBERRY]
  Write down, "Prince John a villain." Why, this is flat perjury to
  call a prince's brother villain.

BORACHIO
  Master Constable–

[DOGBERRY]
  Pray thee, fellow, peace! I do not like thy look, I promise thee.   35

SEXTON
  What heard you him say else?

SECOND WATCHMAN
  Marry, that he had received a thousand ducats of Don John for
  accusing the Lady Hero wrongfully.

[DOGBERRY]
  Flat burglary as ever was committed.

[VERGES]
  Yea, by th' Mass, that it is.   40

SEXTON
  What else fellow?

FIRST WATCHMAN
  And that Count Claudio did mean upon his words to disgrace
  Hero before the whole assembly and not marry her.

[DOGBERRY]
  O villain! Thou wilt be condemned into everlasting redemption
  for this.   45

SEXTON
  What else?

FIRST WATCHMAN
  This is all.

53: **opinioned:** he means "pinioned" (pinned by the arms)

55: **Coxcomb:** fool

54–55: **Let them be...Coxcomb!:** The folio reads: Let them be in the hands of Cox-combe." William Warburton (1747) suggested that the compositor misread the manuscript and offered the following correction:

> **Sexton:** Let them be in hand.
> **Conr.:** Off Coxcomb!

56: **God's:** God save

57: **naughty:** perhaps meaning "motley" or "ill-dressed"; thus, his boast that he is a man who owns "two gowns and everything handsome about him"

58: **varlet:** knave, rascal

63: **piety:** he means "impiety"

John Gilbert as Dogberry, ca. 1863
By permission of the Folger Shakespeare Library

SEXTON
  And this is more, masters, than you can deny. Prince John is this
  morning secretly stolen away; Hero was in this manner accused,
  in this very manner refused, and upon the grief of this suddenly   50
  died. Master Constable, let these men be bound and brought to
  Leonato's. I will go before and show him their examination.

[DOGBERRY]
  Come, let them be opinioned.

SEXTON
  Let them be in the hands of–

[CONRAD]
  Coxcomb!   55

[DOGBERRY]
  God's my life! Where's the Sexton? Let him write down "The
  Prince's Officer Coxcomb." Come, bind them. Thou naughty
  varlet–

[CONRAD]
  Away! You are an ass. You are an ass!

[DOGBERRY]
  Dost thou not suspect my place? Dost thou not suspect my years?   60
  O, that he were here to write me down an ass! But masters,
  remember that I am an ass, though it be not written down, yet
  forget not [that] I am an ass. No, thou villain, thou art full of piety
  as shall be proved upon thee by good witness. I am a wise fellow,
  and, which is more, an officer, and, which is more, a house-holder,   65
  and, which is more, as pretty a piece of flesh as any is in Messina.
  And one that knows the law, go to, and a rich fellow enough, go
  to, and a fellow that hath had losses, and one that hath two
  gowns, and everything handsome about him. Bring him away.
  O that I had been writ down an ass!   70

                                                                      Exeunt

[Much Ado About Nothing Act 5

2-3: to second grief against yourself: to wish your own death

11: Measure his woe...breadth of mine: Let his grief be equal to mine.

12: strain: feeling

16: And sorrow, wag, cry "Hem": There is a surprising amount of suggested correction for this line. The third folio (1664), Nicholas Rowe (1709), and Alexander Pope (2e, 1728) print "And hallow, wag, cry hem"; Joseph Hanmer (1744) emended the line to read: "And sorrowing, cry hem"; Edward Capell (1768) emended "And" to "Bid"; Edmond Malone (1790) preferred "Cry–sorrow, wag!" The line works well as is: Leonato is not content to merely feel his sorrow or to express it by wagging his head or crying aloud.

18: candle-wasters: A candle water is someone who sits up at night, thus burning candles; in this case, one sleepless with grief.

24: preceptial: instructive (precepts = principles or set of rules)

25: Fetter: shackle, tie

28: wring: writhe, suffer

Act 5, Scene 1]

Enter LEONATO and his brother, [ANTHONIO]

[ANTHONIO]
    If you go on thus, you will kill yourself,
    And 'tis not wisdom thus to second grief
    Against yourself.

LEONATO
               I pray thee cease thy counsel,
    Which falls into mine ears as profitless
    As water in a sieve. Give not me counsel,   5
    Nor let no comforter delight mine ear,
    But such a one whose wrongs do suit with mine.
    Bring me a father that so loved his child,
    Whose joy of her is overwhelmed like mine,
    And bid him speak of patience;   10
    Measure his woe the length and breadth of mine,
    And let it answer every strain for strain,
    As thus for thus, and such a grief for such,
    In every lineament, branch, shape, and form.
    If such a one will smile and stroke his beard,   15
    And sorrow, wag, cry "Hem" when he should groan,
    Patch grief with proverbs, make misfortune drunk
    With candle-wasters, bring him yet to me,
    And I of him will gather patience.
    But there is no such man, for, brother, men   20
    Can counsel and speak comfort to that grief,
    Which they themselves not feel, but, tasting it,
    Their counsel turns to passion, which before
    Would give preceptial med'cine to rage,
    Fetter strong madness in a silken thread,   25
    Charm ache with air and agony with words.
    No, no, 'tis all men's office to speak patience
    To those that wring under the load of sorrow,

29: **sufficiency:** ability

30: **moral:** patient

32: **advertisement:** public pronouncements

34: "I pray thee, peace, I will be flesh and blood, / For there was never yet philosopher / That could endure the toothache patiently": Ralph Cosham as Antonio and
Michael Santo as Leonato in the Shakespeare Theatre Company's 2002-2003
production directed by Mark Lamos
Photo: Carol Rosegg

35-36: **For there was...toothache patiently:** Stoic philosophers counseled that man
should endure the griefs and sorrows of this world.

38: **push:** (interjection) pish, pshaw; **made a push:** expressed contempt or disgust;
sufferance: suffering

But no man's virtue nor sufficiency
To be so moral when he shall endure   30
The like himself. Therefore, give me no counsel.
My griefs cry louder than advertisement.

[ANTHONIO]
Therein do men from children nothing differ.

LEONATO
I pray thee, peace, I will be flesh and blood,
For there was never yet philosopher   35
That could endure the toothache patiently,
However they have writ the style of gods
And made a push at chance and sufferance.

[ANTHONIO]
Yet bend not all the harm upon yourself;
Make those that do offend you suffer too.   40

LEONATO
There thou speak'st reason, nay I will do so.
My soul doth tell me Hero is belied,
And that shall Claudio know; so shall the Prince,
And all of them that thus dishonor her.

                              Enter DON PEDRO and CLAUDIO

[ANTHONIO]
Here comes the Prince and Claudio hastily.   45

DON PEDRO
Good den, good den.

CLAUDIO
                    Good day to both of you.

LEONATO
Hear you, my lords?

DON PEDRO
                    We have some haste Leonato—

49: **all is one:** i.e., it doesn't matter

52: **Some of us:** i.e., Claudio and Don Pedro; **lie low:** be prostrate (from being attacked or killed)

52: Stage Direction: *puts his hand on his sword*: a sign that he is ready to fight

55: **beshrew:** a mild curse

58: **fleer:** smirk

59: **dotard:** weak-brained, demented

62: **to thy head:** to your face

64: **lay my reverence by:** dispense with the authority or respect accorded to me by my age

LEONATO
  Some haste, my lord? Well, fare you well, my lord,
  Are you so hasty now? Well, all is one.

DON PEDRO
  Nay, do not quarrel with us, good old man.   50

ANTHONIO
  If he could right himself with quarrelling,
  Some of us would lie low.

CLAUDIO
                    Who wrongs him?
                    [CLAUDIO puts his hand on his sword]

LEONATO
  Marry, thou dost wrong me, thou dissembler, thou.
  Nay, never lay thy hand upon thy sword,
  I fear thee not.

CLAUDIO
                    Marry, beshrew my hand   55
  If it should give your age such cause of fear.
  In faith, my hand meant nothing to my sword.

LEONATO
  Tush, tush, man, never fleer and jest at me,
  I speak not like a dotard nor a fool,
  As under priviledge of age to brag   60
  What I have done, being young, or what would do,
  Were I not old. Know, Claudio, to thy head,
  Thou hast so wronged mine innocent child and me
  That I am forced to lay my reverence by,
  And, with gray hairs and bruise of many days,   65
  Do challenge thee to trial of a man.
  I say thou hast belied mine innocent child.
  Thy slander hath gone through and through her heart,
  And she lies buried with her ancestors,
  O, in a tomb where never scandal slept,   70
  Save this of hers, framed by thy villainy.

75: **nice fence:** skill at fencing

76: **lustihood:** vigor

78: **daffe:** usually modernized to "doff," but "daffe" is the present tense of "daft," used at 2.3.143

82: **Win me and wear me:** Defeat me and then treat me as you like.

84: **foining fence:** fencing thrust; to "foin" means to thrust with a pointed weapon

90: **Boys...milk-sops:** insults, perhaps meant to goad Claudio into accepting his challenge

CLAUDIO
　My villainy?

LEONATO
　　　　　Thine Claudio, thine I say.

DON PEDRO
　You say not right, old man.

LEONATO
　　　　　My lord, my lord,
　I'll prove it on his body, if he dare.
　Despite his nice fence and his active practice,　　　　　　　　75
　His May of youth and bloom of lustihood.

CLAUDIO
　Away, I will not have to do with you.

LEONATO
　Canst thou so daffe me? Thou hast killed my child.
　If thou kill'st me, boy, thou shalt kill a man.

ANTHONIO
　He shall kill two of us, and men, indeed!　　　　　　　　80
　But that's no matter, let him kill one first.
　Win me and wear me. Let him answer me!
　Come, follow me, boy, come sir boy, come, follow me
　Sir boy, I'll whip you from your foining fence,
　Nay, as I am a gentleman, I will.

LEONATO
　　　　　Brother–　　　　　　　　85

ANTHONIO
　Content yourself. God knows I loved my niece,
　And she is dead, slandered to death by villains
　That dare as well answer a man in deed
　As I dare take a serpent by the tongue.
　Boys, apes, braggarts, Jacks, milk-sops–

Robert Lanchester as Leonato and Larry Swansen as Antonio in The Shakespeare Theatre of New Jersey's 2003 production directed by Bonnie J. Monte
Photo: Gerry Goodstein

90: **Brother Anthony:** Leonato is trying to calm his brother down.

93: **Scambling:** unruly; **out-facing:** defiant or brazen; **fashion-monging:** foppish

95: **anticly:** like a fool, from the word "antic" or "foolish"; see Hamlet's feigned "antic disposition" (1.5)

107: **smart:** hurt

LEONATO

Brother Anthony–   90

ANTHONIO

Hold you content. What man? I know them, yea,
And what they weigh, even to the utmost scruple:
Scambling, out-facing, fashion-monging boys
That lie and cog and flout, deprave, and slander,
Go anticly and show outward hidiousness   95
And speak of half a dozen dang'rous words,
How they might hurt their enemies, if they durst.
And this is all.

LEONATO

But brother Anthony–

ANTHONIO

Come, 'tis no matter,
Do not you meddle. Let me deal in this.   100

DON PEDRO

Gentlemen both, we will not wake your patience.
My heart is sorry for your daughter's death,
But, on my honor, she was charged with nothing
But what was true and very full of proof.

LEONATO

My lord, my lord–

DON PEDRO

I will not hear you.   105

LEONATO

No? Come, brother, away. I will be heard.

ANTHONIO

And shall, or some of us will smart for it.
                    Exeunt all but CLAUDIO and DON PEDRO
                                Enter BENEDICK

108: Scene: In the Public Theater's Central Park *Much Ado About Nothing* (2004), Dominic Chianese portrayed a gallant old Anthonio trying to duel Claudio with his cane.

111: **fray:** fight

112–113: **snapped… old men:** a joke. Since old men have bad teeth, they cannot bite.

117–118: **high proof melancholy:** beyond doubt out of sorts

118: **fain:** gladly

118-119: **Wilt thou use thy wit:** Beatrice did say that the Prince and Claudio consider Benedick to be a jester of sorts (2.1.107).

120: **It is in my scabbard:** i.e., my wit is in my action, not my words; perhaps recalling Beatrice's contempt for men who prefer talk to action (4.1.300-301)

DON PEDRO

See, see, here comes the man we went to seek.

CLAUDIO

Now, signor, what news?

BENEDICK

Good day, my lord.   110

DON PEDRO

Welcome, signor. You are almost come to part almost a fray.

CLAUDIO

We had liked to have had our two noses snapped off with two old men without teeth.

DON PEDRO

Leonato and his brother. What thinkest thou? Had we fought, I doubt we should have been too young for them.   115

BENEDICK

In a false quarrel there is no true valor. I came to seek you both.

CLAUDIO

We have been up and down to seek thee, for we are high proof melancholy and would fain have it beaten away. Wilt thou use thy wit?

BENEDICK

It is in my scabbard. Shall I draw it?   120

DON PEDRO

Doest thou wear thy wit by thy side?

CLAUDIO

Never any did so, though very many have been beside their wit. I will bid thee draw, as we do the minstrels, draw to pleasure us.

DON PEDRO

As I am an honest man, he looks pale. Art thou sick or angry?

125: **care killed a cat:** a proverb, perhaps akin to our modern saying "curiosity killed the cat"

126: **mettle:** spirit

127: **in the career:** at full speed

127-128: **charge it against me:** i.e., use your wit as a weapon and charge at me

129: **staff:** topic on which to make jokes

132: **girdle:** a large belt with buckles, turned around to face the back before wrestling or some other violent encounter; **turn his girdle:** i.e., prepare to fight

135-138: **You are a villain...Let me hear from you:** Often said as an aside, thus explaining the Prince's "What, a feast, a feast?" He thinks they are planning a party.

141: **capon:** poultry, reinforcing the idea of a feast, though it does seem to be an odd time to joke. Clearly, Claudio still does not take Benedick seriously.

142: **curiously:** skillfully

143: **woodcock:** a bird associated with simplicity and folly; used also in *Taming of the Shrew* (1.2)

Costume rendering for Benedick from the 1958 production at the Shakespeare Memorial Theatre directed by Douglas Seale. See photographs from this production on pages 88, 172, and 260.

CLAUDIO

    What, courage, man. What, though care killed a cat, thou hast   125
    mettle enough in thee to kill care.

BENEDICK

    Sir, I shall meet your wit in the career, and you charge it against
    me. I pray you, choose another subject.

CLAUDIO

    Nay, then, give him another staff. This last was broke 'cross.

DON PEDRO

    By this light, he changes more and more; I think he be angry   130
    indeed.

CLAUDIO

    If he be, he knows how to turn his girdle.

BENEDICK

    [Aside to CLAUDIO] Shall I speak a word in your ear?

CLAUDIO

    God bless me from a challenge.

BENEDICK

    [Aside to CLAUDIO] You are a villain. I jest not. I will make it   135
    good how you dare with what you dare and when you dare. Do
    me right, or I will protest your cowardice. You have killed a sweet
    lady, and her death shall fall heavy on you. Let me hear from you.

CLAUDIO

    Well, I will meet you, so I may have good cheer.

DON PEDRO

    What, a feast, a feast?   140

CLAUDIO

    I'faith I thank him. He hath bid me to a calves' head and a capon,
    the which if I do not carve most curiously, say my knife's naught.
    Shall I not find a woodcock too?

148: **Just:** exactly

149: **a wise gentleman:** Beatrice is being sarcastic; she means "a fool."

151: **foreswore:** renounced

153: **trans-shape:** change the shape of

155: **properest:** finest

160: **God saw him…in the garden:** a reference to the gulling scene (2.3) and also to Genesis 3.8: after Adam eats the apple from the tree of knowledge, he and Eve hid themselves "amongst the trees of the garden"

161-164: **But when shall we set…the married man:** reference to Benedick's speech against marriage in 1.1.193-197

166–167: **You break jest…blades:** Braggards damage their blades in private then claim it happened in a fight.

BENEDICK
Sir, your wit ambles well; it goes easily.

DON PEDRO
I'll tell thee how Beatrice praised thy wit the other day. I said 145
thou hadst a fine wit. "True," said she, "a fine little one." "No,"
said I, "a great wit." "Right," says she, "a great gross one." "Nay,"
said I, "a good wit." "Just," said she, "it hurts nobody." "Nay," said
I, "the gentleman is wise." "Certain," said she, "a wise gentleman."
"Nay," said I, "he hath the tongues." "That I believe," said she, 150
"for he swore a thing to me on Monday night, which he forswore
on Tuesday morning. There's a double tongue, there's two
tongues." Thus did she an hour together trans-shape thy particular virtues, yet, at last, she concluded with a sigh, thou wast the
properest man in Italy. 155

CLAUDIO
For the which she wept heartily, and said she cared not.

DON PEDRO
Yea, that she did, but, yet for all that, an if she did not hate him
deadly, she would love him dearly. The old man's daughter told
us all–

CLAUDIO
All, all, and moreover, God saw him when he was hid in the garden. 160

DON PEDRO
But when shall we set the savage bull's horns on the sensible
Benedick's head?

CLAUDIO
Yea, and text underneath, "Here dwells Benedick, the married
man"?

BENEDICK
Fare you well, boy, you know my mind. I will leave you now to 165
your gossip-like humor. You break jests as braggards do their
blades, which God be thanked hurt not. My lord, for your many

179: **He is then a giant to an ape:** The sense here is that Benedick is not thinking clearly. He is captive to his apish, irrational love of Beatrice.

181: **Pluck up:** pluck out; **sad:** serious

184: **cursing:** accursed

courtesies I thank you; I must discontinue your company. Your
brother the Bastard is fled from Messina. You have, among you,
killed a sweet and innocent lady. For my Lord Lackbeard there,   170
he and I shall meet and, till then, peace be with him.

[Exit]

DON PEDRO
He is in earnest.

CLAUDIO
In most profound earnest and, I'll warrant you, for the love of
Beatrice.

DON PEDRO
And hath challenged thee.   175

CLAUDIO
Most sincerely.

DON PEDRO
What a pretty thing man is when he goes in his doublet and hose
and leaves off his wit.

CLAUDIO
He is then a giant to an ape, but then is an ape a doctor to such a
man.   180

DON PEDRO
But soft you, let me be. Pluck up my heart and be sad. Did he not
say my brother was fled?
        Enter DOGBERRY, CONRAD, and BORACHIO [and WATCH]

DOGBERRY
Come you, sir, if justice cannot tame you, she shall ne'er weigh
more reasons in her balance. Nay, an you be a cursing hypocrite
once, you must be looked to.   185

DON PEDRO
How now, two of my brother's men bound? Borachio one.

tracks 35-37

188-220
Bruce Armstrong as Claudio, Ron Hastings as Don Pedro,
William Fulton as Dogberry, and Edwin Rubin as Borachio
Robin Phillips as Claudio, Anthony Nicholls as Don Pedro,
Colin Ellis as Dogberry, and Peter Birrel as Borachio

187: **Harken:** inquire

190: **slanders:** he means "slanderers"

191: **verified:** asserted

199: **This learned...to be understood:** The Prince is making a joke, suggesting that Dogberry's language is so confusing as to be virtually incomprehensible.

202: "I have deceived even your very eyes.": Thom Marriott as Borachio, Robert King as Conrad, and Sanjay Talwar, Brian Hamman, Andrew Massingham, Sean Baek, Johnathan Gould, and Shaun McComb as members of the Watch in the Stratford Festival of Canada's 2006 production directed by Douglas Lemcke
Photo: Richard Bain; Courtesy: Stratford Festival of Canada Archives

CLAUDIO
Harken after their offense, my lord.

DON PEDRO
Officers, what offense have these men done?

DOGBERRY
Marry sir, they have committed false report; moreover, they have
spoken untruths; secondarily they are slanders; sixth and lastly,   190
they have belied a lady; thirdly, they have verified unjust things
and, to conclude, they are lying knaves.

DON PEDRO
First, I ask thee what they have done; thirdly, I ask thee what's
their offense; sixth and lastly, why they are committed and, to
conclude, what you lay to their charge.   195

CLAUDIO
Rightly reasoned, and in his own division and, by my troth,
there's one meaning well suited.

DON PEDRO
Who have you offended, masters, that you are thus bound to your
answer? This learned Constable is too cunning to be understood.
What's your offense?   200

BORACHIO
Sweet Prince, let me go no farther to mine answer. Do you hear me,
and let this Count kill me. I have deceived even your very eyes.
What your wisdoms could not discover, these shallow fools have
brought to light, who, in the night, overheard me confessing to this
man how Don John, your brother, incensed me to slander the lady   205
Hero, how you were brought into the orchard and saw me court
Margaret in Hero's garments, how you disgraced her when you
should marry her. My villainy they have upon record, which I had
rather seal with my death than repeat over to my shame. The lady
is dead upon mine and my master's false accusation and, briefly, I   210
desire nothing but the reward of a villain.

tracks 35-37

188-220

Bruce Armstrong as Claudio, Ron Hastings as Don Pedro,
William Fulton as Dogberry, and Edwin Rubin as Borachio
Robin Phillips as Claudio, Anthony Nicholls as Don Pedro,
Colin Ellis as Dogberry, and Peter Birrel as Borachio

215: **the practice of it:** i.e., carrying it out

216: **framed of treachery:** naturally designed to commit treacherous acts

220: **plaintiffs:** he means "defendants"

221: **reformed:** he means "informed"

223: Stage Direction: ***Enter LEONATO, his Brother [ANTHONIO], and the SEXTON:*** the folio has Leonato entering alone

227: "If you would know your wronger, look on me.": Michael Tisdale as Conrad, Michael Polak as Borachio and Peter Rini as Don Pedro in the Shakespeare Theatre Company's 2002-2003 production directed by Mark Lamos
Photo: Carol Rosegg

DON PEDRO
Runs not this speech like iron through your blood?

CLAUDIO
I have drunk poison whiles he uttered it.

DON PEDRO
But did my brother set thee on to this?

BORACHIO
Yea, and paid me richly for the practice of it.   215

DON PEDRO
He is composed and framed of treachery
And fled he is upon this villainy.

CLAUDIO
Sweet Hero, now thy image doth appear
In the rare semblance that I loved it first.

DOGBERRY
Come, bring away the plaintiffs. By this time our Sexton hath   220
reformed Signor Leonato of the matter. And masters, do not forget
to specify, when time and place shall serve, that I am an ass.

CONRAD
Here, here comes master Signor Leonato and the Sexton too.
        Enter LEONATO, his Brother [ANTHONIO], and the SEXTON

LEONATO
Which is the villain? Let me see his eyes
That, when I note another man like him,   225
I may avoid him. Which of these is he?

BORACHIO
If you would know your wronger, look on me.

LEONATO
Art thou the slave that with thy breath hast killed
Mine innocent child?

230: **beliest thyself:** tell lies about yourself

238: **Impose me:** i.e., impose on me

242: **any heavy weight:** any hard punishment, perhaps recalling the twelve labors of Hercules (2.1.275)

246: **Possess:** make known to

248: **aught:** at all

249: **epitaph:** traditional poems read by friends at the grave of the departed

255: **she alone...both of us:** in 1.2.1, Anthonio has a son

BORACHIO
                Yea, even I alone.

LEONATO
  No, not so villain, thou beliest thyself.   230
  Here stand a pair of honorable men,
  A third is fled that had a hand in it.
  I thank you Princes for my daughter's death.
  Record it with your high and worthy deeds.
  'Twas bravely done, if you bethink you of it.   235

CLAUDIO
  I know not how to pray your patience,
  Yet I must speak. Choose your revenge yourself,
  Impose me to what penance your invention
  Can lay upon my sin, yet sinned I not,
  But in mistaking.

DON PEDRO
                By my soul, nor I,   240
  And yet to satisfy this good old man,
  I would bend under any heavy weight
  That he'll enjoin me to.

LEONATO
  I cannot bid you bid my daughter live.
  That were impossible, but, I pray you both,   245
  Possess the people in Messina here
  How innocent she died and, if your love
  Can labor aught in sad invention,
  Hang her an epitaph upon her tomb
  And sing it to her bones, sing it tonight.   250
  Tomorrow morning, come you to my house
  And, since you could not be my son-in-law,
  Be yet my nephew. My brother hath a daughter,
  Almost the copy of my child that's dead,
  And she alone is heir to both of us.   255
  Give her the right you should have giv'n her cousin,
  And so dies my revenge.

262: **naughty:** wicked (a much stronger sense than current usage)

267: **But always hath been just and virtuous:** Borachio's defense of Margaret is odd. It's difficult to conceive how she could have been virtuous considering their "vile encounters" (4.1.87). This remark may tell us more about Borachio's character and his willingness to shoulder all blame than it does about Margaret's sexual innocence.

269: **white and black:** the black ink written upon white paper

272: **one "Deformed":** Dogberry has apparently been speaking to the Second Watchman (see 3.3.96).

280: **There's for thy pains:** Leonato gives Dogberry a reward, probably of money.

CLAUDIO
> O noble sir!
Your overkindness doth wring tears from me.
I do embrace your offer and dispose
For henceforth of poor Claudio.   260

LEONATO
Tomorrow, then, I will expect your coming;
Tonight, I take my leave. This naughty man
Shall face-to-face be brought to Margaret,
Who I believe was packed in all this wrong,
Hired to it by your brother.

BORACHIO
> No, by my soul, she was not,   265
Nor knew not what she did when she spoke to me,
But always hath been just and virtuous,
In anything that I do know by her.

DOGBERRY
Moreover, sir, which, indeed, is not under white and black, this
plaintiff here, the offendor, did call me "ass." I beseech you, let it   270
be remembered in his punishment, and also the Watch heard
them talk of one "Deformed." They say he wears a key in his ear
and a lock hanging by it, and borrows money in God's name, the
which he hath used so long and never paid that now men grow
hard-hearted and will lend nothing for God's sake. Pray you,   275
examine him upon that point.

LEONATO
I thank thee for thy care and honest pains.

DOGBERRY
Your worship speaks like a most thankful and reverend youth,
and I praise God for you.

LEONATO [Gives him money]
There's for thy pains.   280

284: correct yourself: Leonato should punish the prisoner, but, in Dogberry's ill construction, it sounds like Leonato should punish himself.

286: I humbly give you leave to depart: he means "I humbly *ask* your leave to depart "

287: prohibit: he means "permit"

DOGBERRY
God save the foundation.

LEONATO
Go, I discharge thee of thy prisoner, and I thank thee.

DOGBERRY
I leave an arrant knave with your worship, which I beseech your
worship to correct yourself for the example of others. God keep
your worship. I wish your worship well. God restore you to   285
health. I humbly give you leave to depart, and if a merry meeting
may be wished, God prohibit it. Come neighbor–

LEONATO
Until tomorrow morning, lords, farewell.
               [Exeunt DOGBERRY, BORACHIO, CONRAD, and WATCH]

ANTHONIO
Farewell, my lords, we look for you tomorrow.

DON PEDRO
We will not fail.   290

CLAUDIO
Tonight, I'll mourn with Hero.

LEONATO
Bring you these fellows on. We'll talk with Margaret, how her
acquaintance grew with this lewd fellow.
                                                         Exeunt

tracks 38-39

1-15
Samuel West as Benedick and Amanda Root as Margaret

2: **to the speech of:** with my speech to

4: **In so high a style:** pun on "stile," steps built to go over a fence

6-7: **keep below stairs:** a pun on maids and maidenhead or virginity. Maids stay downstairs (in the servants' quarters), and "maid" also means "virgin" (4.1.79). Thus, if she remains a virgin, then no man will have ever come over (i.e., lain on top of) her.

8: **Thy wit...it catches:** Since greyhounds are fast, they catch their prey.

12–14: **swords...bucklers...pikes...dangerous weapons:** double entendres. Margaret makes a correspondence between swords/bucklers and the male/female sexual organs. Benedick builds on the pun by bringing up "pikes," a central spike affixed to the buckler by a screw. They are dangerous to maids in the sense of violating virginity.

Act 5, Scene 2]

Enter BENEDICK and MARGARET

BENEDICK
  Pray thee, sweet Mistress Margaret, deserve well at my hands by
  helping me to the speech of Beatrice.

MARGARET
  Will you then write me a sonnet in praise of my beauty?

BENEDICK
  In so high a style, Margaret, that no man living shall come over
  it, for, in most comely truth, thou deservest it.   5

MARGARET
  To have no man come over me? Why, shall I always keep below
  stairs?

BENEDICK
  Thy wit is as quick as the greyhound's mouth; it catches.

MARGARET
  And yours as blunt as the fencer's foils, which hit, but hurt not.

BENEDICK
  A most manly wit, Margaret; it will not hurt a woman. And so I   10
  pray thee, call Beatrice. I give thee the bucklers.

MARGARET
  Give us the swords. We have bucklers of our own.

BENEDICK
  If you use them, Margaret, you must put in the pikes with a vice,
  and they are dangerous weapons for maids.

1-15
Samuel West as Benedick and Amanda Root as Margaret

20: **Leander:** From Greek mythology, Leander swam across the Hellespont to be with his lover, Hero.

21: **Troilus:** In Shakespeare's play, *Troilus and Cressida* (ca.1601-3), Troilus engaged Pander to help him seduce Cressida.

22: **quondam:** former

23: **rod:** as in ruler, here compared to the measured feet of poetic meter, though the word is often modernized to "road," a very different reading

26: **horn:** a sign of sexual infidelity (referring to a cuckold's horns)

27-29: "No, I was not born under a rhyming planet, nor I cannot woo in festival terms.": Michael Redgrave as Benedick in the 1958 RSC production directed by Douglas Seale
Photo: Angus McBean © Royal Shakespeare Company

28-29: **festival:** festive, joyful

29: Stage Direction: ***Enter BEATRICE:*** The quarto has Beatrice entering a line later.

MARGARET
  Well, I will call Beatrice to you, who, I think, hath legs.   15
                                                   Exit MARGARET

BENEDICK
  And therefore will come.
  [Reads his sonnet]
          The God of love that sits above, and knows me,
          and knows me,
          how piti-ful I deserve–

  I mean in singing, but in loving. Leander the good swimmer,   20
  Troilus the first employer of pandars, and a whole book full of
  these quondam carpet-mongers, whose names yet run smoothly in
  the even rod of a blank verse, why they were never so truly turned
  over and over as my poor self in love. Marry, I cannot show it in
  rhyme. I have tried, I can find out no rhyme to "lady" but "baby,"   25
  an innocent rhyme; for "scorn," "horn," a hard rhyme; for
  "school," "fool," a babbling rhyme. Very ominous endings. No, I
  was not born under a rhyming planet, nor I cannot woo in festival terms.
                                                   Enter BEATRICE
  Sweet Beatrice, wouldst thou come when I called thee?   30

BEATRICE
  Yea, Signor, and depart when you bid me.

BENEDICK
  O stay but till then–

BEATRICE
  "Then" is spoken. Fare you well now. And yet, ere I go, let me go
  with that I came, which is with knowing what hath past between
  you and Claudio.   35

BENEDICK
  Only foul words, and, thereupon, I will kiss thee.

37: **foul wind:** bad breath, or possibly flatulence. Since he smells, she will not kiss him.

38: **noisome:** offensive, noxious

42: **subscribe him a coward:** announce to the world that he is a coward

55: **An old, an old:** the compositor may have inadvertently set the text twice, rather than this being a repetition on Benedick's part

56: **erect...his own tomb:** protect or build his own reputation

57-58: **he shall live...the widow weeps:** i.e., he will be forgotten quickly

BEATRICE

Foul words is but foul wind, and foul wind is but foul breath, and
foul breath is noisome. Therefore, I will depart unkissed.

BENEDICK

Thou hast frighted the word out of his right sense, so forcible is
thy wit. But I must tell thee plainly, Claudio undergoes my   40
challenge, and either I must shortly hear from him, or I will
subscribe him a coward. And, I pray thee, now tell me, for which
of my bad parts didst thou first fall in love with me?

BEATRICE

For them all together, which maintained so politic a state of evil
that they will not admit any good part to intermingle with them.   45
But for which of my good parts did you first suffer love for me?

BENEDICK

Suffer love! A good epithet, I do suffer love, indeed, for I love thee
against my will.

BEATRICE

In spite of your heart, I think. Alas, poor heart, if you spite it for
my sake, I will spite it for yours, for I will never love that which   50
my friend hates.

BENEDICK

Thou and I are too wise to woo peaceably.

BEATRICE

It appears not in this confession. There's not one wise man among
twenty that will praise himself.

BENEDICK

An old, an old instance Beatrice, that lived in the time of good   55
neighbors. If a man do not erect in this age his own tomb ere he
dies, he shall live no longer in monument than the bell rings and
the widow weeps.

60: **Question:** he means "What a foolish question"; **a quarter:** a quarter of an hour; **rheum:** weeping

61: **Don Worm:** conscience was often depicted as a worm or serpent

66: **ill:** badly

71: **old coil:** much turmoil

73: **abused:** fooled

76-77: "I will live in thy heart...and, moreover, I will go with thee to thy uncle's.": Derek Jacobi as Benedick and Sinead Cusack as Beatrice in the 1982 RSC production directed by Terry Hands
Photo: Donald Cooper

BEATRICE
And how long is that, think you?

BENEDICK
Question, why an hour in clamor and a quarter in rheum. Therefore   60
is it most expedient for the wise, if Don Worm, his conscience, find
no impediment to the contrary, to be the trumpet of his own virtues,
as I am to myself so much for praising myself, who, I myself will
bear witness, is praiseworthy. And now, tell me, how doth your
cousin?   65

BEATRICE
Very ill.

BENEDICK
And how do you?

BEATRICE
Very ill too.

BENEDICK
Serve God, love me, and mend. There will I leave you too, for here
comes one in haste.   70
Enter URSULA

URSULA
Madam, you must come to your uncle. Yonder's old coil at home.
It is proved my lady Hero hath been falsely accused, the Prince
and Claudio mightily abused, and Don John is the author of all,
who is fled and gone. Will you come presently?

BEATRICE
Will you go hear this news, signor?   75

BENEDICK
I will live in thy heart, die in thy lap and be buried in thy eyes, and,
moreover, I will go with thee to thy uncle's.
Exeunt

5: guerdon: payment

12: *[BALTHASAR]*: Claudio calls for someone to sing. Since Balthasar has already sung a song at 2.3.55, it makes sense that he perform here as well.

PARDON·GODDESS·OF THE·NIGHT   ACT·V·SC·III

12: "Pardon, goddess of the night": Engraving by Byam Shaw, from 1900
By permission of the Folger Shakespeare Library

13: virgin knight: a pun on knight/night. The fame of Hero, whose name suggests the virtues of a knight, was killed in the night. See also *All's Well that Ends Well*: "Dian no queen of virgins, that would suffer her poor knight surprised, without rescue" (1.3).

16: Midnight assist our moan, help us to sigh and groan: often cut into two lines, but this is the quarto and folio lineation

19: be uttered: be spoken of

Act 5, Scene 3]

Enter CLAUDIO, DON PEDRO and three or four
[ATTENDANTS] with tapers

CLAUDIO
  Is this the monument of Leonato?

LORD
  It is, my lord.
  [Hangs epitaph and reads]
      Done to death by slanderous tongues,
      Was the Hero that here lies.
      Death, in guerdon of her wrongs,   5
      Gives her fame which never dies.
      So the life that died with shame
      Lives in death with glorious fame.
      Hang thou there upon the tomb,
      Praising her when I am dead.   10

CLAUDIO
  Now, music sound and sing your solemn hymn.

[BALTHASAR]
  Song.
      Pardon, goddess of the night,
      Those that slew thy virgin knight,
      For the which, with songs of woe,
      Round about her tomb they go.   15
      Midnight assist our moan, help us to sigh and groan.
      Heavily, heavily.
      Graves yawn and yield your dead,
      Till death be uttered,
      Heavily, heavily.   20

21: Now unto...this rite: Both quarto and folio assign this line to "Lord." Nicholas Rowe (1709) assigned it to Claudio, and almost all editions since have followed suit.

23: preyed: hunted, but the audience may think Claudio is saying "prayed"

24: Phoebus: Apollo, who pulls the sun round the earth

27: "Good morrow, masters, each his several way": Barrett Foa as Claudio in the Shakespeare Theatre Company's 2002-2003 production directed by Mark Lamos
Photo: Carol Rosegg

27: several: separate

28: weeds: mourning clothes

30: Hymen: God of Marriage

[CLAUDIO]
Now unto thy bones good night; yearly will I do this rite.

DON PEDRO
Good morrow, masters, put your torches out.
The wolves have preyed and, look, the gentle day
Before the wheels of Phoebus, round about
Dapples the drowsy east with spots of grey.   25
Thanks to you all and leave us. Fare you well.

CLAUDIO
Good morrow, masters, each his several way.

DON PEDRO
Come, let us hence and put on other weeds,
And then to Leonato's we will go.

CLAUDIO
And Hymen now with luckier issue speeds   30
Than this for whom we rendered up this woe.

Exeunt

3: **debated:** discussed

5: **against her will:** perhaps, unintentionally

6: **question:** investigation

14: **office:** duty

17: **confirmed countenance:** carefully controlled expression

Enter LEONATO, BENEDICK MARGARET URSULA,
[ANTHONIO], FRIAR, HERO [and Ladies]

FRIAR
Did I not tell you she was innocent?

LEONATO
So are the Prince and Claudio, who accused her
Upon the error that you heard debated.
But Margaret was in some fault for this,
Although against her will, as it appears,   5
In the true course of all the question.

[ANTHONIO]
Well, I am glad that all things sorts so well.

BENEDICK
And so am I, being else by faith enforced
To call young Claudio to a reckoning for it.

LEONATO
Well, daughter, and you, gentlewomen, all,   10
Withdraw into a chamber by yourselves,
And when I send for you, come hither masked.
The Prince and Claudio promised by this hour
To visit me. You know your office, brother.
You must be father to your brother's daughter,   15
And give her to young Claudio.

Exeunt Ladies

[ANTHONIO]
Which I will do with confirmed countenance.

BENEDICK
Friar, I must entreat your pains, I think.

20: **To bind me or undo me:** to marry me or ruin me

27: **Your answer, sir, is enigmatical:** Why Benedick should be puzzled is equally puzzling, since the Prince and Claudio have already confessed that they know all about his love of Beatrice (5.1.163).

FRIAR
  To do what, signor?

BENEDICK
  To bind me or undo me, one of them.   20
  Signor Leonato, truth it is, good signor,
  Your niece regards me with an eye of favor.

LEONATO
  That eye my daughter lent her, 'tis most true.

BENEDICK
  And I do with an eye of love requite her.

LEONATO
  The sight whereof I think you had from me,   25
  From Claudio, and the Prince, but what's your will?

BENEDICK
  Your answer, sir, is enigmatical.
  But for my will, my will is your good will
  May stand with ours this day to be conjoined
  In the state of honorable marriage,   30
  In which, good Friar, I shall desire your help.

LEONATO
  My heart is with your liking.

FRIAR
                    And my help.
                    Enter DON PEDRO and CLAUDIO, with two or
                    three more [ATTENDANTS]

  Here comes the Prince and Claudio.

DON PEDRO
  Good morrow to this fair assembly.

38: **I'll hold my mind:** i.e., I won't change my mind; **Ethiope:** someone with a dark complexion, which was considered unattractive at the time

41: **February face:** cold, frosty face

43: **savage bull:** reference to 1.1.193

45-46: **Europa...Europa:** the first time, a reference to the continent; the second, to the myth of Europa, who slept with Jove when that deity took the form of a bull

49-51: **And some strange bull...his bleat:** Europa's child, King Minos, was a bastard. Benedick suggests that Claudio's mother did as Europa did; thus, Claudio is a bastard.

Barrett Foa as Claudio, Edwin C. Owens as Friar Francis, and Kathleen Early as Hero in the Shakespeare Theatre Company's 2002-2003 production directed by Mark Lamos

Photo: Carol Rosegg

LEONATO

    Good morrow, Prince, good morrow, Claudio.   35
    We here attend you. Are you yet determined
    Today to marry with my brother's daughter?

CLAUDIO

    I'll hold my mind, were she an Ethiope.

LEONATO

    Call her forth, brother. Here's the Friar ready.

DON PEDRO

    Good morrow, Benedick. Why, what's the matter   40
    That you have such a February face,
    So full of frost, of storm, and cloudiness?

CLAUDIO

    I think he thinks upon the savage bull.
    Tush, fear not, man, we'll tip thy horns with gold,
    And all Europa shall rejoice at thee,   45
    As once Europa did at lusty Jove,
    When he would play the noble beast in love.

BENEDICK

    Bull Jove, sir, had an amiable low,
    And some such strange bull leapt your father's cow,
    And got a calf in that same noble feat   50
    Much like to you, for you have just his bleat.
                Enter [ANTHONIO], HERO [veiled],
                BEATRICE, MARGARET, URSULA

CLAUDIO

    For this, I owe you. Here comes other reckonings.
    Which is the lady I must seize upon?

LEONATO

    This same is she, and I do give you her.

63: **defiled:** slandered

67: **qualify:** mitigate

70: **let wonder seem familiar:** i.e., act as if these extraordinary events are commonplace or ordinary

tracks 40-42

72-96
John Horton as Benedick, Maureen Fitzgerald as Beatrice,
Budd Knapp as Leonato, Bruce Armstrong as Claudio, and Faith Ward as Hero
Richard Johnson as Benedick, Pauline Jameson as Beatrice,
Newton Blick as Leonato, Robin Phillips as Claudio, and Annette Crosbie as Hero

73: "I answer to that name. What is your will?": Engraving by James Fittler, from 1795
By permission of the Folger Shakespeare Library

CLAUDIO
Why then, she's mine. Sweet, let me see your face— 55

LEONATO
No, that you shall not, till you take her hand
Before this Friar and swear to marry her.

CLAUDIO
Give me your hand before this holy Friar;
I am your husband if you like of me.

HERO *[Removing veil]*
And when I lived I was your other wife, 60
And when you loved, you were my other husband.

CLAUDIO
Another Hero?

HERO
                    Nothing certainer.
One Hero died defiled, but I do live,
And surely as I live, I am a maid.

DON PEDRO
The former Hero—Hero that is dead? 65

LEONATO
She died, my lord, but whiles her slander lived.

FRIAR
All this amazement can I qualify
When, after that the holy rites are ended,
I'll tell you largely of fair Hero's death.
Meantime, let wonder seem familiar, 70
And to the chapel let us presently.

BENEDICK
Soft and fair, Friar, which is Beatrice?

72-96
John Horton as Benedick, Maureen Fitzgerald as Beatrice,
Budd Knapp as Leonato, Bruce Armstrong as Claudio, and Faith Ward as Hero
Richard Johnson as Benedick, Pauline Jameson as Beatrice,
Newton Blick, Robin Phillips as Claudio, and Annette Crosbie as Hero

82: **'Tis no such matter:** i.e., that is not true

83: **friendly recompense:** equal to your friendly love

84: **cousin:** also a term for a close friend or relation

Ellen Terry as Beatrice
By permission of the Folger Shakespeare Library

BEATRICE *[Unveiling]*
I answer to that name. What is your will?

BENEDICK
Do not you love me?

BEATRICE
Why no, no more than reason.

BENEDICK
Why then your uncle, and the Prince, and Claudio   75
Have been deceived; they swore you did.

BEATRICE
Do not you love me?

BENEDICK
Troth, no, no more than reason.

BEATRICE
Why, then, my Cousin Margaret and Ursula
Are much deceived, for they did swear you did.

BENEDICK
They swore that you were almost sick for me.   80

BEATRICE
They swore that you were well-nigh dead for me.

BENEDICK
'Tis no such matter; then you do not love me?

BEATRICE
No, truly, but in friendly recompense.

LEONATO
Come, cousin, I am sure you love the gentleman.

tracks 40-42

72-96

John Horton as Benedick, Maureen Fitzgerald as Beatrice,
Budd Knapp as Leonato, Bruce Armstrong as Claudio, and Faith Ward as Hero
Richard Johnson as Benedick, Pauline Jameson as Beatrice,
Newton Blick, Robin Phillips as Claudio, and Annette Crosbie as Hero

92: **by this light:** i.e., to speak truly, here meant lightheartedly

95: **consumption:** a withering sickness, tuberculosis

96: **I will stop your mouth:** I will stop your talking by kissing you.

Jimmy Smits as Benedick and Kristen Johnston as Beatrice in The Public Theater
2004 production directed by David Esbjornson
Photo: Michal Daniel

97: Scene: **Benedick, the married man:** In 1749, David Garrick played Benedick soon
after his own wedding to the Viennese dancer Eva Maria Veigel.

99–100: **satire or epigram:** humorous insults

103: **for what:** from the folio; the quarto prints "for"

104: **giddy:** unpredictable

CLAUDIO

And I'll be sworn upon't that he loves her,   85
For here's a paper written in his hand:
A halting sonnet of his own pure brain,
Fashioned to Beatrice.

HERO

                                    And here's another,
Writ in my cousin's hand, stol'n from her pocket,
Containing her affection unto Benedick.   90

BENEDICK

A miracle. Here's our own hands against our hearts. Come, I will
have thee, but, by this light, I take thee for pity.

BEATRICE

I would not deny you, but, by this good day, I yield upon great
persuasion, and, partly to save your life, for I was told you were
in a consumption.   95

BENEDICK

Peace, I will stop your mouth.

                                                            [Kisses her]

DON PEDRO

How dost thou, Benedick, the married man?

BENEDICK

I'll tell thee what Prince. A college of wit-crackers cannot flout
me out of my humor. Dost thou think I care for a satire or an
epigram? No, if a man will be beaten with brains, a shall wear   100
nothing handsome about him. In brief, since I do purpose to
marry, I will think nothing to any purpose that the world can say
against it, and therefore never flout at me for what I have said
against it, for man is a giddy thing, and this is my conclusion.
[Kisses Beatrice] For thy part Claudio, I did think to have beaten   105
thee, but in that thou art like to be my kinsman, live unbruised
and love my cousin.

109: **cudgelled:** beaten

109–110: **a double-dealer:** a rule breaker, unfaithful

116–117: **there is no staff...tipped with horn:** In ancient Cretan festivals, single men used staffs to jump over bulls. The meaning here is that the Prince would do well to marry, even if he runs the risk of being gored by a bull.

120: **brave punishments:** a rather dark way to end a comedy, but not unusual in the Shakespeare canon (see Aaron's fate in *Titus Andronicus* or Iago's fate in *Othello*)

120: Scene: John Barton's RSC production (1976), the play ended with Judi Dench's Beatrice holding Benedick's sword while he joined in a dance.

Judi Dench as Beatrice, Robin Ellis as Don Pedro, and Ensemble in the 1976 RSC production directed by John Barton

Photo: Donald Cooper

CLAUDIO

I had well hoped thou wouldst have denied Beatrice, that I might
have cudgelled thee out of thy single life to make thee a double-
dealer, which, out of question, thou wilt be, if my cousin do not   110
look exceeding narrowly to thee.

BENEDICK

Come, come, we are friends. Let's have a dance ere we are
married that we may lighten our own hearts and our wives' heels.

LEONATO

We'll have dancing afterward.

BENEDICK

First, of my word, therefore play music. Prince, thou art sad? Get   115
thee a wife, get thee a wife; there is no staff more reverend then
one tipped with horn.

Enter MESSENGER

MESSENGER

My Lord, your brother John is ta'en in flight
And brought with armed men back to Messina.

BENEDICK

Think not on him till tomorrow. I'll devise thee brave punishments   120
for him. Strike up pipers!

Dance [and Exeunt]

The Cast Speaks

THE 2006 CAST FROM THE STRATFORD FESTIVAL OF CANADA

Marie Macaisa

In the text of the play, directors, actors, and other interpreters of Shakespeare's work find a wealth of information to portray. For example, in *Much Ado About Nothing* we hear that Benedick is a "good soldier" and "hath done good service" in the war and that Claudio is an exceptional soldier who "hath borne himself beyond the promise of his age." Hero is, according to Claudio, "the sweetest lady that ever I looked on," and Beatrice, as described by Don Pedro, is "a pleasant, spirited lady," who, Leonato says, has "little of the melancholy element in her...[and] is never sad but when she sleeps and not ever sad then." As for the villain, we recognize him immediately upon entry: he is referred to in the stage direction as *"JOHN THE BASTARD."* (In Shakespeare, "bastards" often suggest both dubious parentage and a dark temperament.)

Intriguingly, Shakespeare (like all playwrights and unlike novelists) also leaves gaps. We're not exactly sure how Beatrice and Benedick came to have such a relationship, though there are clues. And we also don't know the reason for Don John's machinations. We are coaxed to fill in the missing information ourselves, either through reasonable surmises (we can guess that Beatrice and Benedick had a previous relationship from Beatrice's response to Leonato about losing the heart of Signior Benedick: "Indeed, my lord, he lent it me awhile, and I gave him use for it" 2.1.212) or through back stories we supply on our own (perhaps Benedick broke Beatrice's heart). This mix, simultaneously knowing too much and not enough, enables us to paint vivid, varied interpretations of the same play.

In staging a play, directors create a vision for their production based on the text but also move beyond that by making decisions on what isn't in the text. In collaboration with actors, they flesh out the characters: they discuss what they might be like, they create stories that explain their actions, they determine motivations, and they speculate on the nature of their relationships. In Shakespeare they have a rich text to draw on and hundreds of years of performances for inspiration. Thus we, the audience, can experience a play anew each time we see a different production. Perhaps it is in an unfamiliar setting, perhaps it is in a scene or characterization we hadn't noticed in the past, perhaps it is in the realization that we have changed our opinions about the actions of the characters in the play. Whatever the case, a closer look into one cast's interpretation creates an opportunity for us to make up our own minds about their stories and, in the process, gain new insights not only into a play hundreds of years old, but also quite possibly ourselves.

STRATFORD FESTIVAL OF CANADA, 2006

Though this production of *Much Ado About Nothing* is set in Messina, the backdrop is the Edwardian era, the years from 1901-1910, roughly corresponding to the reign of King Edward VII in Great Britain. That era, marked by abundance and an enthusiasm for the art and fashion of the European continent, is often referred to as the "Gilded Age." The style of that period inspired the visual world of the production, but its focus is firmly on the interior: the relationships that permeate the play.

This interview was conducted in August 2006, in the middle of the run of the production. The actors were interviewed individually about their characters, their relationships, and important scenes. Keep in mind that their answers represent but one interpretation of the play. You may be surprised; you may agree or disagree strongly with a point of view. That is exactly the point.

ON CLAUDIO AND HERO

Jeffrey Wetsch: Claudio

Claudio is a young man in transition to adulthood. He's a lover, similar to Romeo in some ways: he's emotional; he falls in love very quickly. However, he's not as confident as Romeo and he's somewhat paranoid. He's still young; he needs to make mistakes and learn from them.

I think Claudio and Hero have seen each other only briefly before. He says himself that before he left for the war, he "looked upon her with a soldier's eye" meaning he liked her but saw her in a different light. Their relationship is mostly silent, as opposed to Beatrice and Benedick's.

Adrienne Gould: Hero

Hero is also very emotional. She doesn't volunteer much on her own but is instead constantly reacting: to Claudio, to Beatrice, to her father. She feels a sense of duty to her father and also a strong attachment. He feels the same way—in fact, he gives her the choice to marry or at least prepare herself for his proposal ("But I will acquaint my daughter withal, that she may be the better prepared for an answer.").

We learn a lot about Hero in her scene (3.4) before the wedding. Though she doesn't say much when men are around, in this scene with Ursula, Margaret, and her cousin, she flashes some feistiness. She declares to Margaret, "My cousin's a fool, and thou art another," when she disagrees about her wardrobe. I do think this is also a time when she feels, subconsciously, the absence of her mother. We don't know what happened to her; she's just not around. She has some kind of foreboding that things aren't going to go well: "God give me joy to wear it, for my heart is exceeding heavy."

Peter Donaldson as Benedick in the Stratford Festival of Canada's 2006 production directed by Stephen Ouimette
Photo: Richard Bain; Courtesy: Stratford Festival of Canada Archives

ON BENEDICK

Peter Donaldson: Benedick

Benedick hasn't grown up. He's been shirking his responsibilities for quite a while in pursuit of the finer things in life. He's happy; he thinks it's easier to live the way he does than take on the complications of living with a woman. He and Claudio and Don Pedro are a band of brothers.

Shane Carty: Don Pedro

Don Pedro and Benedick have been friends for a long time. Benedick is a lot of fun to have around. He's intelligent, they are both soldiers, they are roughly in the same position in the world, and having him [Benedick] as part of his entourage is a relief to him. It was difficult for royalty to be informal and joke around with friends, so he's happy to have Benedick with him.

Peter Donaldson: Benedick

It riles Benedick to hear Beatrice describe him as the Prince's jester, because he knows that's partly what he is.

Lucy Peacock as Beatrice in the Stratford Festival of Canada's 2006 production directed by Stephen Ouimette
Photo: Richard Bain; Courtesy: Stratford Festival of Canada Archives

ON BEATRICE

Lucy Peacock: Beatrice

I think she's accepted where she is in life, even if it is rather like, though not exactly, a compromise. She has accepted the possibility that she will not have a true love, a partner in life, without melancholy. The thing that keeps her going and breathing, I believe, is her wit.

In that household, she has an audience to react to her, to reflect her, and she needs that. She's not the kind of the character who would act in front of the mirror. If she didn't have anyone listening, I don't think she would speak. What she doesn't realize is that she's taken it too far. During the gulling scene (3.1), it's revealed to her that her wit is not her best trait, and she always thought it was. She thinks it's what makes her attractive, alive. She sees it as charming and challenging, in a positive way. And she discovers then that it's not!

That criticism cuts very deep. But what's brilliant about her is that she chooses to rise above it. Immediately. She decides to have a huge life change right that second; no more of the scornful, disdainful Beatrice.

ON BEATRICE AND BENEDICK

Peter Donaldson: Benedick

We know that there's been a situation in their past, some unfinished business, that has displeased both of them. At the end of one of their battles, as I walk away, she says, "You always end with a jade's trick. I know you of old." (1.1.107). Maybe it's about him not wanting to commit, I don't know. But there is something unresolved. In the gulling scene (2.3.83-180), when he overhears the men talk about Beatrice's passionate love for him, he feels that this gives him the upper hand and it frees him to pursue her. I think if someone had told him directly that Beatrice felt that way, he would not have believed it.

Lucy Peacock: Beatrice

I think they had a miscommunication that hurt them both deeply; it's possible that she thinks that Benedick hurt her by offering some kind of connection or commitment and then going AWOL on it, one way or another. Whether he had to go to war, never said goodbye and left things unresolved, she assumed that he was not a man of his word and that it was all over. Conversely, Benedick might have thought that Beatrice had given him an indication but didn't follow through on it and felt betrayed. Then there is the possibility that both Beatrice and Benedick think that the other one is responsible for the breakdown. They're both hurt, they think the other person is fully to blame, and they can't communicate. That's very human. They are both proud and stubborn people; neither will be the one to give in.

Don Pedro, Don John, Borachio, and Margaret

When we first meet Claudio, Benedick, Don Pedro, and Don John ("John the Bastard" in the stage direction), they are returning from a war. We don't know much about it, but we do know Benedick and Claudio are soldiers in the army led by Don Pedro, and we learn in the first scene that they were victorious. Don John's role in the war is not clarified.

Shane Carty: Don Pedro

As the Prince, he has the highest status in the play. In my mind, his going off to war and this consequent visit to Messina is his last adventure, his last chance to escape responsibility. He is leaving alone at the end of the play to go back to Aragon to resume his duties.

He has known Leonato for a long time and they have great affection for each other. I think Leonato and Don Pedro's father were very close and they've visited each other many times. Don Pedro and Benedick have also been friends for a while. He likes having Benedick in his entourage: he's fun, he's intelligent, and he's of an acceptable social standing. Claudio he has known for the shortest amount of time, but he is his best soldier and he probably considers him his protégé. He sees that Claudio is impulsive and suspects that he won't handle the situation with Hero properly, so he generously offers to woo her for him. I think he also thinks it would be fun.

Wayne Best: Don John

Don John is the illegitimate brother of Don Pedro. As a character, Don John is underwritten and we don't know much about what motivates him to act the way he does (though there are clues in the text). But this is not a play about Don John and his purposes. As an actor, I need to surrender to what

Shane Carty as Don Pedro in the Stratford Festival of Canada's 2006 production
directed by Stephen Ouimette
Photo: Richard Bain; Courtesy: Stratford Festival of Canada Archives

Shakespeare wanted: for Don John to be the villain and catalyst for what happens.

Yet, I did think about the sources for his resentment. First, because he is illegitimate he can't inherit, so his brother gets the honor. Also, in our production, they cast Don Pedro younger than Don John. So, Don John sees this younger man (someone who became the Prince instead of him) behaving inappropriately and frivolously (he's a crowned head and he spends his time finding dates for his friends?!), and he finds this revolting. We also talked about the war from which they had just come being an attempted coup d'état by Don John. It was unsuccessful, and though he's been allowed back with the group, he's been warned to behave.

Why does he hate Leonato so much? I can understand why he hates his brother and why he hates Claudio (who has supplanted him as the number two man to the Prince). I can understand that: All Leonato has done is welcome him (1.1.114-115): "Let me bid you welcome, my lord, being reconciled to the Prince, your brother." Yet, from the perspective of the character, everyone else has politely ignored mentioning his troubles, and here Leonato is announcing it to the world. How dare he? And he even makes a joke about bastards: he responds to Don Pedro's "I think this is your daughter" with "Her mother hath many times told me so." (1.1.77-78) There's a bastard standing right there and he's making a joke.

But really, Shakespeare doesn't care why Don John is the way he is. As an actor, I can base the performance on those ideas or on something like his having very bad migraine headaches his whole life. All that's important is that I fulfill the character's dramatic function and that is to be the catalyst.

One of Don John's men, and his fellow conspirator, is Borachio. In this production, he is made a gentleman, though of lower stature than Don John.

Thom Marriott: Borachio

Borachio is an ambitious young man who has attached himself to Don John in an effort to better his social standing. In many productions, he is played as a drunk ["borracho" is the Spanish word for "drunk"; it is "ubriaco" in Italian], which I did not do, and I fought for that choice quite a bit. I don't think Borachio is the one who's drunk; I think he's the intoxicant for Don John. He's the little devil on his shoulder saying "We can do this, we can make things go horribly wrong."

Why? He's a first-generation gentleman, not from old money like Leonato. He's a social climber, constantly trying to better his own life by hooking up with people who have money. "For when rich villains have need of poor ones, poor ones may make what price they will." (3.3.86-87) One thousand ducats is a year's salary for him; of course he's going to help Don John.

Borachio tells Don Jon how much he is "in the favor of Margaret, the waiting gentlewoman to Hero" and hatches the scheme whereby he and Margaret are observed from a distance in an amorous encounter. He is overheard calling her "Hero," and she calling him "Claudio" (though changed to "Borachio" in this production to make it more understandable to the audience). Thus Hero, far from being the sweet, virginal young lady, appears to be promiscuous and unfaithful.

Nicolá Correia-Damude: Margaret

I think Margaret's relationship with Borachio is genuine, which you see from his defense of her when the plot is discovered. [Borachio responds to Leonato's accusation of Margaret by denying her involvement and telling him she "knew not what she did when she spoke to me, / But always hath been just and virtuous, / In anything that I do know by her" (5.1.266-268).] In a way it's like a modern relationship; it's almost like they were dating, if there was an equivalent of a boyfriend in those times.

I strongly believe that Margaret never imagined that what she was doing with Borachio would in any way affect Hero. I think her love for Hero is genuine and she wouldn't do anything to hurt her. She and the other women in the play are really each other's family: they live close together in a community and have a sisterly bond. What's so shocking and confusing is why she would jeopardize that, why she would allow Borachio to use her. That's why I think she doesn't know about the plot.

In her banter with Benedick (5.2), when she asks him "Why, shall I always keep below stairs?," I think perhaps there's a jealousy of Hero. Hero is almost like a sister to her, yet she, Margaret, will never be a princess. She's always that step below, and she feels that she's worthy of more, so I think there's something attractive to her in playing Hero. Borachio suggests role-playing, and there's a part of her that thinks it's exciting and almost the fulfillment of a dream. I do think her playing Hero in that moment is not just out of envy but also out of admiration, love, and wanting to be her and to please him. She would love to be Hero for a day.

Borachio and Don John's scheme works, and Claudio, spurred by self-right-eous betrayal, publicly denounces Hero as an "approvèd wanton," Don Pedro adding that she is a "common stale," the basest, lowest-class prostitute.

THE WEDDING
Jeffrey Wetsch: Claudio

Claudio fell utterly in love with Hero very quickly. Being emotional, very young, and not very confident, when he thinks he has been betrayed, it is as if his world has ended. He reacts as a hot-blooded young man, shaming her in the most public way possible and totally destroying her.

Jeffrey Wetsch as Claudio in the Stratford Festival of Canada's 2006 production
directed by Stephen Ouimette
Photo: Richard Bain; Courtesy: Stratford Festival of Canada Archives

Ian Deakin: Friar Francis

I think he's just as shocked as anybody else. All of sudden Claudio goes mad
in the church. I assume his accusation isn't true because I know the family.
I watch her face and see the blushes: "I have marked a thousand blushing
apparitions / To start into her face, a thousand innocent shames, / In angel
whiteness beat away those blushes" (4.1.152-154). When I ask her point-
blank (and I'm the only one who asks her), "What man is he you are accused
of?," she tells me she doesn't know.

I liken Friar Francis to another famous friar in Shakespeare: Friar Laurence. I think of him as a young Laurence, one who hasn't made terrible mistakes. This may have been one of the very first wedding ceremonies he
conducted, and he's picked the wrong one. He has to take control because it's
completely out of hand, and luckily, the idea comes to him in a flash. There
are no potions involved, like the ones Laurence is famous for. He comes up
with the plan to cloister Hero in order for time to go by, heal things, and give
everyone a chance to come to their senses. He counsels Leonato to "hang

mournful epitaphs, and do all rites / That appertain unto a burial (4.1.200-201). In his big speech (4.1.203-236), he assures everyone that no matter what happens, it's going to work out for the best. He gives them a great deal of hope. It's an acting challenge to spin the plot and encourage the hope.

Peter Donaldson: Benedick

Benedick learns a lesson from watching Claudio tear apart Hero and seeing Beatrice's reaction to it. He goes after her, and in their scene (4.1.248-311) he realizes just how horribly men treat women and how ridiculous their earlier behavior had been. When he confronts Claudio and Don Pedro about Hero dying, he is doing so also for those personal reasons, in addition to complying with Beatrice's wishes.

DOGBERRY AND THE WATCH

The plot to disrupt the wedding is uncovered by a most surprising group: the malapropism-spouting Dogberry, constable of Messina, and his rag-tag crew. Had they not come along, the play might have been a tragedy.

Robert Persichini: Dogberry

Dogberry and the Watch, I believe, have other jobs and that theirs are volunteer positions, kind of like a fire brigade. When something comes up, they take care of whatever needs to be done. I'm not exactly sure whether he and his men know each other but I play the scene as if they are new and Dogberry hasn't seen them before. He's dismayed and had hoped for a better team. He's enormously proud of his badge, and he wears a suit and tie. The rest of the Watch has just come in from the field; they are a rag-tag bunch.

From my point of view, he has a rock solid belief in his own competence and intelligence. In playing the character you have to believe that. He uses his astonishing vocabulary, of which he is again enormously proud, to impress.

The excitement for him develops over the course of four scenes. First, he has to give the Watch instructions on what to do in certain situations. His men respond by asking about hypothetical outcomes (e.g., What if the drunks refuse your order to go home to bed? What if the vagrants disobey their order to stand?). Though he's unsure of what to do, he thinks on his feet and answers with extreme confidence.

In the following scene, they actually find the two villains and uncover the plot. His zenith is the trial scene. He tries to tell Leonato about the plot, but Leonato, busy preparing for the wedding, tells him to take care of it himself. For Dogberry it's his chance. He sends Verges to get the Sexton because he has a pen and they need a transcript of the trial.

Don Carrier: Sexton

The Sexton is not only associated with the church also has a connection with the judiciary in this small town. Dogberry represents the arm of the police and he's a bit like a judge, though not one who could pass sentences. He's more a kind of notary of that time.

Though he's often played by much older actors and for comedy, in this production we didn't choose either. He does, in fact, represent the voice of reason in the scene he's in. Dogberry, the Watch, and the mayhem around them exasperate him, so he tries to cut through that. We tried different approaches in rehearsal but this worked the best. He's told in this trial scene about a girl who died, and it's not appropriate to be funny.

Robert Persichini: Dogberry

The trial scene is where Dogberry really arrives. The uncovering of the plot is a big deal, and they save the day. It reinforces his absolute belief in right and wrong. He has a moral compass, he takes his job seriously, and he has great pride in himself and his appearance. "To be a well-favored man is a gift of Fortune," he says, referring to himself (3.3.10).

The way Dogberry mangles language is juxtaposed against the incredible wordplay of Beatrice and Benedick, whose language sparkles. There's something in that counterpoint. Here are Beatrice and Benedick, people who have a great facility with language, and yet they can't get it together. Then along comes Dogberry, someone who doesn't speak all that well, and he gets it all done. The whole mess gets untangled, and the play ends with music and dancing.

EPILOGUE
So do Beatrice and Benedick live happily ever after? The actors speculate:

Peter Donaldson: Benedick

I think they will be gloriously happy! They were made for each other. Benedick also realizes that they've both wasted a lot of time they could have spent with each other, so he'll spend the rest of their lives making up for that.

Lucy Peacock: Beatrice

Their marriage? It will be fabulous! They'll continue to challenge each other and love each other deeply. They will be deliriously happy in the most perfect way: an absolute partnership. They'll cook breakfast together; they'll travel around the world together. They will still yell and scream at each other, but it end with a kiss, or a giggle, and just an added appreciation of each other.

In the church scene, the Friar talks about how Claudio will realize what he missed when he thinks Hero is dead and goes on to add that this happens so much in life: "That what we have we prize not to the worth / Whiles we enjoy it, but, being lacked and lost, / Why then we rack the value" (4.1.211-213). That gets Beatrice thinking and she takes a little peek at Benedick. She realizes it then, I think, just moments before he says, "I love you."

Lucy Peacock as Beatrice in the Stratford Festival of Canada's 2006 production directed by Stephen Ouimette
Photo: Richard Bain; Courtesy: Stratford Festival of Canada Archives

A Voice Coach's Perspective on Speaking Shakespeare

KEEPING SHAKESPEARE PRACTICAL

Andrew Wade

Introduction to Speaking Shakespeare: Derek Jacobi
Speaking Shakespeare: Andrew Wade with Santino Fontana

tracks 43–44

Why, you might be wondering, is it so important to keep Shakespeare practical? What do I mean by practical? Why is this the way to discover how to speak the text and understand it?

Plays themselves are not simply literary events—they demand interpreters in the deepest sense of the word, and the language of Shakespeare requires, therefore, not a vocal demonstration of writing techniques but an imaginative response to that writing. The key word here is imagination. The task of the voice coach is to offer relevant choices to the actor so that the actor's imagination is titillated, excited by the language, which he or she can then share with an audience, playing on that audience's imagination. Take the word "IF"—it is only composed of two letters when written, but if you say it aloud and listen to what it implies, then your reaction, the way the word plays through you, can change the perception of meaning. "Ifffffffff"... you might hear and feel it implying "possibilities," "choices," "questioning," "trying to work something out." The saying of this word provokes active investigation of thought. What an apt word to launch a play: "If music be the food of love, play on" (Act 1, Scene 1 in *Twelfth Night, or What You Will*). How this word engages the listener and immediately sets up an involvement is about more than audibility. How we verbalize sounds has a direct link to meaning and understanding. In the words of Touchstone in *As You Like It*, "Much virtue in if."

I was working with a company in Vancouver on *Macbeth,* and at the end of the first week's rehearsal—after having explored our voices and opening out different pieces of text to hear the possibilities of the rhythm, feeling how the meter affects the thinking and feeling, looking at structure and form—one of the actors admitted he was also a writer of soap operas and that I had completely changed his way of writing. Specifically, in saying a line like, "The multitudinous seas incarnadine / Making the green one red" he heard the complexity of meaning revealed in the use of polysyllabic words becoming monosyllabic, layered upon the words' individual dictionary definitions. The writer was reminded that merely reproducing the speech of everyday life was nowhere near as powerful and effective as language that is shaped.

Do you think soap operas would benefit from rhyming couplets? Somehow this is difficult to imagine! But, the writer's comments set me thinking. As I am constantly trying to find ways of exploring the acting process, of opening out actors' connection with language that isn't their own, I thought it would be a good idea to involve writers and actors in some practical work on language. After talking to Cicely Berry (Voice Director, the Royal Shakespeare Company) and Colin Chambers (the then RSC Production Adviser), we put together a group of writers and actors who were interested in taking part. It was a fascinating experience all round, and it broke down barriers and misconceptions.

The actors discovered, for instance, that a writer is not coming from a very different place as they are in their creative search; that an idea or an image may result from a struggle to define a gut feeling and not from some crafted, well-formed idea in the head. The physical connection of language to the body was reaffirmed. After working with a group on Yeats' poem *Easter 1916*, Ann Devlin changed the title of the play she was writing for the Royal Shakespeare Company to *After Easter*. She had experienced the poem read aloud by a circle of participants, each voice becoming a realization of the shape of the writing. Thus it made a much fuller impact on her and caused her thinking to shift. Such practical exchanges, through language work and voice, feed and stimulate my work to go beyond making sure the actors' voices are technically sound.

It is, of course, no different when we work on a Shakespeare play. A similar connection with the language is crucial. Playing Shakespeare, in many ways, is crafted instinct. The task is thus to find the best way to tap into someone's imagination. As Peter Brook put it: "People forget that a text is dumb. To make it speak, one must create a communication machine. A living network, like a nervous system, must be made if a text which comes from far away is to touch the sensibility of the present."

This journey is never to be taken for granted. It is the process that every text must undergo every time it is staged. There is no definitive rehearsal that would solve problems or indicate ways of staging a given play. Again, this is where creative, practical work on voice can help forge new meaning by offering areas of exploration and challenge. The central idea behind my work comes back to posing the question, "How does meaning change by speaking out aloud?" It would be unwise to jump hastily to the end process for, as Peter Brook says, "Shakespeare's words are records of the words that he wanted spoken, words issuing from people's mouths, with pitch, pause and rhythm and gesture as part of their meaning. A word does not start as a word—it is the end product which begins as an impulse, stimulated by attitude and behavior which dictates the need for expression." (1)

PRACTICALLY SPEAKING

Something happens when we vocalize, when we isolate sounds, when we start to speak words aloud, when we put them to the test of our physicality, of our anatomy. We expose ourselves in a way that makes taking the language back more difficult. Our body begins a debate with itself, becomes alive with the vibrations of sound produced in the mouth or rooted deep in the muscles that aim at defining sound. In fact, the spoken words bring into play all the senses, before sense and another level of meaning are reached.

"How do I know what I think, until I see what I say," Oscar Wilde once said. A concrete illustration of this phrase was reported to me when I was leading a workshop recently. A grandmother said the work we had done that day reminded her of what her six-year-old grandson had said to his mother while they were driving through Wales: "Look, mummy, sheep! Sheep! Sheep!" "You don't have to keep telling us," the mother replied, but the boy said, "How do I know they're there, if I don't tell you?!"

Therefore, when we speak of ideas, of sense, we slightly take for granted those physical processes which affect and change their meaning. We tend to separate something that is an organic whole. In doing so, we become blind to the fact that it is precisely this physical connection to the words that enables the actors to make the language theirs.

The struggle for meaning is not just impressionistic theater mystique; it is an indispensable aspect of the rehearsal process and carries on during the life of every production. In this struggle, practical work on Shakespeare is vital and may help spark creativity and shed some light on the way meaning is born into language. After a performance of *More Words*, a show devised and directed by Cicely Berry and myself, Katie Mitchell (a former artistic director of The Other Place in Stratford-upon-Avon) gave me an essay by Ted Hughes that echoes with the piece. In it, Ted Hughes compares the writing of a poem—the coming into existence of words—to the capture of a wild animal. You will notice that in the following passage Hughes talks of "spirit" or "living parts" but never of "thought" or "sense." With great care and precaution, he advises, "It is better to call [the poem] an assembly of living parts moved by a single spirit. The living parts are the words, the images, the rhythms. The spirit is the life which inhabits them when they all work together. It is impossible to say which comes first, parts or spirit."

This is also true of life in words, as many are connected directly to one or several of our senses. Here Hughes talks revealingly of "the five senses," of "word," "action," and "muscle," all things which a practical approach to language is more likely to allow one to perceive and do justice to.

Words that live are those which we hear, like "click" or "chuckle," or which we see, like "freckled" or "veined," or which we taste, like "vinegar" or "sugar," or touch, like "prickle" or "oily," or smell, like "tar" or "onion," words which belong to one of the five senses. Or words that act and seem to use their muscles, like "flick" or "balance." (2)

In this way, practically working on Shakespeare to arrive at understanding lends itself rather well, I think, to what Adrian Noble (former artistic director of the RSC) calls "a theater of poetry," a form of art that, rooted deeply in its classical origins, would seek to awaken the imagination of its audiences through love and respect for words while satisfying our eternal craving for myths and twice-told tales.

This can only be achieved at some cost. There is indeed a difficult battle to fight and hopefully win "the battle of the word to survive." This phrase was coined by Michael Redgrave at the beginning of the 1950s, a period when theater began to be deeply influenced by more physical forms, such as mime. (3) Although the context is obviously different, the fight today is of the same nature.

LISTENING TO SHAKESPEARE

Because of the influence of television, our way of speaking as well as listening has changed. It is crucial to be aware of this. We can get fairly close to the way *Henry V* or *Hamlet* was staged in Shakespeare's time; we can try also to reconstruct the way English was spoken. But somehow, all these fall short of the real and most important goal: the Elizabethan ear. How did one "hear" a Shakespeare play? This is hardest to know. My personal view is that we will probably never know for sure. We are, even when we hear a Shakespeare play or a recording from the past, bound irrevocably to modernity. The Elizabethan ear was no doubt different from our own, as people were not spoken to or entertained in the same way. A modern voice has to engage us in a different way in order to make us truly listen in a society that seems to rely solely on the belief that image is truth, that it is more important to show than to tell.

Sometimes, we say that a speech in Shakespeare, or even an entire production, is not well-spoken, not up to standard. What do we mean by that? Evidently, there are a certain number of "guidelines" that any actor now has to know when working on a classical text. Yet, even when these are known, actors still have to make choices when they speak. A sound is not a sound without somebody to lend an ear to it: rhetoric is nothing without an audience.

There are a certain number of factors that affect the receiver's ear. These can be cultural factors such as the transition between different acting styles or the level of training that our contemporary ear has had. There are also personal and emotional factors. Often we feel the performance was not well-spoken because, somehow, it did not live up to our expectations of how we think it should have been performed. Is it that many of us have a self-conscious model, perhaps our own first experience of Shakespeare, that meant something to us and became our reference point for the future (some treasured performance kept under glass)? Nothing from then on can quite compare with that experience.

Most of the time, however, it is more complex than nostalgia. Take, for example, the thorny area of accent. I remind myself constantly that audibility is not embedded in Received Pronunciation or Standard American. The familiarity that those in power have with speech and the articulate confidence gained from coming from the right quarters can lead us all to hear certain types of voices as outshining others. But, to my mind, the role of theater is at least to question these assumptions so that we do not perpetuate those givens but work towards a broader tolerance.

In Canada on a production of *Twelfth Night*, I was working with an actor who was from Newfoundland. His own natural rhythms in speaking seemed completely at home with Shakespeare's. Is this because his root voice has direct links back to the voice of Shakespeare's time? It does seem that compared to British dialects, which are predominantly about pitch, many North American dialects have a wonderful respect and vibrancy in their use of vowels. Shakespeare's language seems to me very vowel-aware. How useful it is for an actor to isolate the vowels in the spoken words to hear the music they produce, the rich patterns, their direct connection to feelings. North Americans more easily respond to this and allow it to feed their speaking. I can only assume it is closer to how the Elizabethans spoke.

In *Othello* the very names of the characters have a direct connection to one vowel in particular. All the male names, except the Duke, end in the sound OH: Othello, Cassio, Iago, Brabantio, etc. Furthermore, the sound OH ripples through the play both consciously and unconsciously. "Oh" occurs repeatedly and, more interestingly, is contained within other words: "so," "soul," and "know." These words resonate throughout the play, reinforcing another level of meaning. The repeating of the same sounds affects us beyond what we can quite say.

Vowels come from deep within us, from our very core. We speak vowels before we speak consonants. They seem to reveal the feelings that require the consonants to give the shape to what we perceive as making sense.

Working with actors who are bilingual (or ones for whom English is not the native language) is fascinating because of the way it allows the actor to have an awareness of the cadence in Shakespeare. There seems to be an objective perception to the musical patterns in the text, and the use of alliteration and assonance are often more easily heard not just as literary devices, but also as means by which meaning is formed and revealed to an audience.

Every speech pattern (i.e., accent, rhythm) is capable of audibility. Each has its own music, each can become an accent when juxtaposed against another. The point at which a speech pattern becomes audible is in the dynamic of the physical making of those sounds. The speaker must have the desire to get through to a listener and must be confident that every speech pattern has a right to be heard.

SPEAKING SHAKESPEARE

So, the way to speak Shakespeare is not intrinsically tied to a particular sound; rather, it is how a speaker energetically connects to that language. Central to this is how we relate to the form of Shakespeare. Shakespeare employs verse, prose, and rhetorical devices to communicate meaning. For example, in *Romeo and Juliet*, the use of contrasts helps us to quantify Juliet's feelings: "And learn me how to lose a winning match," "Whiter than new snow upon a raven's back." These extreme opposites, "lose" and "winning," "new snow" and "raven's back," are her means to express and make sense of her feelings.

On a more personal note, I am often reminded how much, as an individual, I owe to Shakespeare's spoken word. The rather quiet and inarticulate schoolboy I once was found in the speaking and the acting of those words a means to quench his thirst for expression.

NOTES:

(1) Peter Brook, *The Empty Space* (Harmondsworth: Penguin, 1972)
(2) Ted Hughes, *Winter Pollen* (London: Faber and Faber, 1995)
(3) Michael Redgrave, *The Actor's Ways and Means*
    (London: Heinemann, 1951)

In the Age of Shakespeare

Thomas Garvey

One of the earliest published pictures of Shakespeare's birthplace, from an original watercolor by Phoebe Dighton (1834)

The works of William Shakespeare have won the love of millions since he first set pen to paper some four hundred years ago, but at first blush, his plays can seem difficult to understand, even willfully obscure. There are so many strange words: not fancy, exactly, but often only half-familiar. And the very fabric of the language seems to spring from a world of forgotten assumptions, a vast network of beliefs and superstitions that have long been dispelled from the modern mind.

In fact, when "Gulielmus filius Johannes Shakespeare" (Latin for "William, son of John Shakespeare") was baptized in Stratford-on-Avon in 1564, English itself was only just settling into its current form; no dictionary had yet been written, and Shakespeare coined hundreds of words himself. Astronomy and medicine were entangled with astrology and the occult arts; democracy was waiting to be reborn; and even educated people believed in witches and fairies, and that the sun revolved around the Earth. Yet somehow Shakespeare still speaks to us today, in a voice as fresh and direct as the day his lines were first spoken, and to better understand both their artistic depth and enduring power, we must first understand something of his age.

REVOLUTION AND RELIGION

Shakespeare was born into a nation on the verge of global power, yet torn by religious strife. Henry VIII, the much-married father of Elizabeth I, had

From *The Book of Martyrs* (1563), this woodcut shows the Archbishop of Canterbury being burned at the stake in March 1556

Map of London ca. 1625

defied the Pope by proclaiming a new national church, with himself as its head. After Henry's death, however, his daughter Mary reinstituted Catholicism via a murderous nationwide campaign, going so far as to burn the Archbishop of Canterbury at the stake. But after a mere five years, the childless Mary also died, and when her half-sister Elizabeth was crowned, she declared the Church of England again triumphant.

In the wake of so many religious reversals, it is impossible to know which form of faith lay closest to the English heart, and at first, Elizabeth was content with mere outward deference to the Anglican Church. Once the Pope hinted her assassination would not be a mortal sin, however, the suppression of Catholicism grew more savage, and many Catholics— including some known in Stratford—were hunted down and executed, which meant being hanged, disemboweled, and carved into quarters. Many scholars suspect that Shakespeare himself was raised a Catholic (his father's testament of faith was found hidden in his childhood home). We can speculate about the impact this religious tumult may have had on his plays. Indeed, while explicit Catholic themes, such as the description of Purgatory in *Hamlet*, are rare, the larger themes of disguise and double allegiance are prominent across the canon. Prince Hal offers false friendship to Falstaff in the histories, the heroines of the comedies are forced to disguise themselves as men, and the action of the tragedies is driven by double-dealing villains. "I am not what I am," Iago tells us (and himself) in *Othello*, summing up in a single stroke what may have been Shakespeare's formative social and spiritual experience.

If religious conflict rippled beneath the body politic like some ominous undertow, on its surface the tide of English power was clearly on the rise. The defeat of the Spanish Armada in 1588 had established Britain as a global power; by 1595 Sir Walter Raleigh had founded the colony of Virginia (named for the Virgin Queen), and discovered a new crop, tobacco, which would inspire a burgeoning international trade. After decades of strife and the threat of invasion, England enjoyed a welcome stability. As the national coffers grew, so did London; over the course of Elizabeth's reign, the city would nearly double in size to a population of some 200,000.

Hornbook from Shakespeare's lifetime

A 1639 engraving of a scene from a royal state visit of Marie de Medici depicts London's packed, closely crowded half-timbered houses.

FROM COUNTRY TO COURT

The urban boom brought a new dimension to British life—the mentality of the metropolis. By contrast, in Stratford-on-Avon, the rhythms of the rural world still held sway. Educated in the local grammar school, Shakespeare was taught to read and write by a schoolmaster called an "abecedarian", and as he grew older, he was introduced to logic, rhetoric, and Latin. Like most schoolboys of his time, he was familiar with Roman mythology and may have learned a little Greek, perhaps by translating passages of the New Testament. Thus while he never attended a university, Shakespeare could confidently refer in his plays to myths and legends that today we associate with the highly educated.

Beyond the classroom, however, he was immersed in the life of the countryside, and his writing all but revels in its flora and fauna, from the wounded deer of *As You Like It* to the herbs and flowers which Ophelia scatters in *Hamlet*. Pagan rituals abounded in the rural villages of Shake-speare's day, where residents danced around maypoles in spring, performed "mummers' plays" in winter, and recited rhymes year-round to ward off witches and fairies.

The custom most pertinent to Shakespeare's art was the medieval "mys-tery play," in which moral allegories were enacted in country homes and vil-lage squares by troupes of traveling actors. These strolling players—usually four men and two boys who played the women's roles—often lightened the moralizing with bawdy interludes in a mix of high and low feeling, which would become a defining feature of Shakespeare's art. Occasionally even a professional troupe, such as Lord Strange's Men, or the Queen's Men, would arrive in town, perhaps coming straight to Shakespeare's door (his father was the town's bailiff) for permission to perform.

Rarely, however, did such troupes stray far from their base in London, the nation's rapidly expanding capital and cultural center. The city itself had existed since the time of the Romans (who built the original London Bridge), but it was not until the Renaissance that its population spilled beyond its ancient walls and began to grow along (and across) the Thames, by whose banks the Tudors had built their glorious palaces. It was these two contradic-tory worlds—a modern metropolis cheek-by-jowl with a medieval court—that provided the two very different audiences who applauded Shakespeare's plays.

Londoners both high and low craved distraction. Elizabeth's court con-stantly celebrated her reign with dazzling pageants and performances that required a local pool of professional actors and musicians. Beyond the grace-ful landscape of the royal parks, however, the general populace was packed into little more than a square mile of cramped and crooked streets where the-atrical entertainment was frowned upon as compromising public morals.

Just outside the jurisdiction of the city fathers, however, across the twenty arches of London Bridge on the south bank of the Thames, lay the wilder district of "Southwark." A grim reminder of royal power lay at the end of the bridge—the decapitated heads of traitors stared down from pikes at passers-by. Once beyond their baleful gaze, people found the amusements they desired, and their growing numbers meant a market suddenly existed for daily entertainment. Bear-baiting and cockfighting flourished, along with taverns, brothels, and even the new institution of the theater.

Southwark, as depicted in Hollar's long view of London (1647). Blackfriars is on the top right and the labels of Bear-baiting and the Globe were inadvertently reversed.

THE ADVENT OF THE THEATRE

The first building in England designed for the performance of plays—called, straightforwardly enough, "The Theatre"—was built in London when Shakespeare was still a boy. It was owned by James Burbage, father of Richard Burbage, who would become Shakespeare's lead actor in the acting company The Lord Chamberlain's Men. "The Theatre," consciously or unconsciously, resembled the yards in which traveling players had long plied their trade—it was an open-air polygon, with three tiers of galleries surrounding a canopied stage in a flat central yard, which was ideal for the athletic competitions the building also hosted. The innovative arena must have found an appreciative audience, for it was soon joined by the Curtain, and then the Rose, which was the first theater to rise in Southwark among the brothels, bars, and bear-baiting pits.

Even as these new venues were being built, a revolution in the drama itself was taking place. Just as Renaissance artists turned to classical models for inspiration, so English writers looked to Roman verse as a prototype for the new national drama. "Blank verse," or iambic pentameter (that is, a poetic line with five alternating stressed and unstressed syllables), was an adaptation of Latin forms, and first appeared in England in a translation of Virgil's *Aeneid*. Blank verse was first spoken on stage in 1561, in the now-forgotten *Gorboduc*, but it was not until the brilliant Christopher Marlowe (born the same year as Shakespeare) transformed it into the "mighty line" of such plays as *Tamburlaine* (1587) that the power and flexibility of the form made it the baseline of English drama.

Marlowe—who, unlike Shakespeare, had attended college—led the "university wits," a clique of hard-living free thinkers who in between all manner of exploits managed to define a new form of theater. The dates of Shakespeare's arrival in London are unknown—we have no record of him in Stratford after 1585—but by the early 1590s he had already absorbed the essence of Marlowe's invention, and begun producing astonishing innovations of his own.

While the "university wits" had worked with myth and fantasy, however, Shakespeare turned to a grand new theme, English history—penning the three-part saga of *Henry VI* in or around 1590. The trilogy was such a success that Shakespeare became the envy of his circle—one unhappy competitor, Robert Greene, even complained in 1592 of "an upstart crow...beautified with our feathers...[who is] in his own conceit the only Shake-scene in a country."

Such jibes perhaps only confirmed Shakespeare's estimation of himself, for he began to apply his mastery of blank verse in all directions, succeeding at tragedy (*Titus Andronicus*), farce (*The Comedy of Errors*), and romantic comedy (*The Two Gentlemen of Verona*). He drew his plots from everywhere: existing poems, romances, folk tales, even other plays. In fact a number of Shakespeare's dramas (*Hamlet* included) may be revisions of earlier texts owned by his troupe. Since copyright laws did not exist, acting companies usually kept their texts close to their chests, only allowing publication when a play was no longer popular, or, conversely, when a play was *so* popular (as with *Romeo and Juliet*) that unauthorized versions had already been printed.

Demand for new plays and performance venues steadily increased. Soon, new theaters (the Hope and the Swan) joined the Rose in Southwark, followed shortly by the legendary Globe, which opened in 1600. (After some trouble with their lease, Shakespeare's acting troupe, the Lord

> pendeſt on ſo meane a ſtay. Baſe minded men all thꝛee
> of you, if by my miſerie you be not warnd: foꝛ vnto none
> of you (like mee) ſought thoſe burres to cleaue: thoſe
> Puppets (I meane) that ſpake from our mouths, thoſe
> Anticks garniſht in our colours. Is it not ſtrange, that
> I, to whom they all haue beene beholding: is it not like
> that you, to whome they all haue beene beholding, ſhall
> (were yee in that caſe as I am now) bee both at once of
> them foꝛſaken? Yes truſt them not: foꝛ there is an vp-
> ſtart Crow, beautified with our feathers, that with his
> Tygers hart wrapt in a Players hyde, ſuppoſes he is as
> well able to bombaſt out a blanke verſe as the beſt of
> you: and beeing an abſolute Iohannes fac totum, is in
> his owne conceit the onely Shake-ſcene in a countrey.
> O that I might intreat your rare wits to be imploied in
> moꝛe pꝛofitable courſes: & let thoſe Apes imitate your
> paſt excellence, and neuer moꝛe acquaint them with
> your admired inuentions. I knowe the beſt huſband of

Greene's insult, lines 9–14

Chamberlain's Men, had disassembled "The Theatre" and transported its timbers across the Thames, using them as the structure for the Globe.) Shakespeare was a shareholder in this new venture, with its motto "All the world's a stage," and continued to write and perform for it as well. Full-length plays were now being presented every afternoon but Sunday, and the public appetite for new material seemed endless.

The only curb on the public's hunger for theater was its fear of the plague—for popular belief held the disease was easily spread in crowds. Even worse, the infection was completely beyond the powers of Elizabethan medicine, which held that health derived from four "humors" or internal fluids identified as bile, phlegm, blood, and choler. Such articles of faith, however, were utterly ineffective against a genuine health crisis, and in times of plague, the authorities' panicked response was to shut down any venue where large crowds might congregate. The theaters would be closed for lengthy periods in 1593, 1597, and 1603, during which times Shakespeare was forced to play at court, tour the provinces, or, as many scholars believe, write what would become his famous cycle of sonnets.

THE NEXT STAGE

Between these catastrophic closings, the theater thrived as the great medium of its day; it functioned as film, television, and radio combined as well as a venue for music and dance (all performances, even tragedies, ended with a dance). Moreover, the theater was the place to see and be seen; for a penny

Famous scale model of the Globe completed by Dr. John Cranford Adams in 1954. Collectively, 25,000 pieces were used in constructing the replica. Dr. Adams used walnut to imitate the timber of the Globe, plaster was placed with a spoon and medicine dropper, and 6,500 tiny "bricks" measured by pencil eraser strips were individually placed on the model.

you could stand through a performance in the yard, a penny more bought you a seat in the galleries, while yet another purchased you a cushion. The wealthy, the poor, the royal, and the common all gathered at the Globe, and Shakespeare designed his plays—with their action, humor, and highly refined poetry—not only to satisfy their divergent tastes but also to respond to their differing points of view. In the crucible of Elizabethan theater, the various classes could briefly see themselves as others saw them, and drama could genuinely show "the age and body of the time his form and pressure," to quote Hamlet himself.

In order to accommodate his expanding art, the simplicity of the Elizabethan stage had developed a startling flexibility. The canopied platform of the Globe had a trap in its floor for sudden disappearances, while an alcove at the rear, between the pillars supporting its roof, allowed for "discoveries" and interior space. Above, a balcony made possible the love scene in *Romeo and Juliet*; while still higher, the thatched roof could double as a tower or rampart. And though the stage was largely free of scenery, the costumes were sumptuous—a theater troupe's clothing was its greatest asset. Patrons were used to real drums banging in battle scenes and real cannons firing overhead (in fact, a misfire would one day set the Globe aflame).

With the death of Elizabeth, and the accession of James I to the throne in 1603, Shakespeare only saw his power and influence grow. James, who considered himself an intellectual and something of a scholar, took over the patronage of the Lord Chamberlain's Men, renaming them the King's Men; the troupe even marched in his celebratory entrance to London. At this pinnacle of both artistic power and prestige, Shakespeare composed *Othello*, *King Lear*, and *Macbeth* in quick succession, and soon the King's Men acquired a new, indoor theater in London, which allowed the integration of more music and spectacle into his work. At this wildly popular venue, Shakespeare developed a new form of drama that scholars have dubbed "the romance," which combined elements of comedy and tragedy in a magnificent vision that would culminate in the playwright's last masterpiece, *The Tempest*. Not long after this final innovation, Shakespeare retired to Stratford a wealthy and prominent gentleman.

Beyond the Elizabethan Universe

This is how Shakespeare fit into his age. But how did he transcend it? The answer lies in the plays themselves. For even as we see in the surface of his drama the belief system of England in the sixteenth century, Shakespeare himself is always questioning his own culture, holding its ideas up to the light and shaking them, sometimes hard. In the case of the Elizabethan faith in astrology, Shakespeare had his villain Edmund sneer, "We make guilty of our disasters the sun, the moon, and stars; as if we were villains on necessity." When pondering the medieval code of chivalry, Falstaff decides, "The better part of valor is discretion." The divine right of kings is questioned in *Richard II*, and the inferior status of women—a belief that survived even the crowning of Elizabeth—appears ridiculous before the brilliant examples of Portia (*The Merchant of Venice*), and Rosalind (*As You Like It*). Perhaps it is through this constant shifting of perspective, this relentless sense of exploration, that the playwright somehow outlived the limits of his own period, and became, in the words of his rival Ben Jonson, "not just for an age, but for all time."

track 45

Conclusion of the Sourcebooks Shakespeare
Much Ado About Nothing: *Derek Jacobi*

About the Online Teaching Resources

The Sourcebooks Shakespeare is committed to supporting students and educators in the study of Shakespeare. A website with additional articles and essays, extended audio, a forum for discussions, and other resources can be found (starting in August 2006) at www.sourcebooksshakespeare.com. To illustrate how the Sourcebooks Shakespeare may be used in your class, Jeremy Ehrlich, the head of education at the Folger Shakespeare Library, contributed an essay called "Working with Audio in the Classroom." The following is an excerpt:

One possible way of approaching basic audio work in the classroom is shown in the handout [on the site]. It is meant to give some guidance for the first-time user of audio in the classroom. I would urge you to adapt this to the particular circumstances and interests of your own students.

To use it, divide the students into four groups. Assign each group one of the four technical elements of audio—volume, pitch, pace, and pause—to follow as you play them an audio clip or clips. In the first section, have them record what they hear: the range they encounter in the clip and the places where their element changes. In the second section, have them suggest words for the tone of the passage based in part on their answers to the first. Sections three and four deal with tools of the actor. Modern acting theory finds the actor's objective is his single most important acting choice; an actor may then choose from a variety of tactics in order to achieve that objective. Thus, if a character's objective on stage is to get sympathy from his scene partner, he may start out by complaining, then shift to another tactic (asking for sympathy directly? throwing a tantrum?) if the first tactic fails. Asking your students to try to explain what they think a character is trying to get, and how she is trying to do it, is a way for them to follow this process through closely. Finally, the handout asks students to think about the meaning (theme) of the passage, concluding with a traditional and important tool of text analysis.

As you can see, this activity is more interesting and, probably, easier for students when it's used with multiple versions of the same piece of text. While defining an actor's motivation is difficult in a vacuum, doing so in relation to another performance may be easier: one Othello may be more concerned with gaining respect, while another Othello may be more concerned with obtaining love, for instance. This activity may be done outside of a group setting, although for students doing this work for the first time I suggest group work so they will be able to share answers on some potentially thought-provoking questions . . .

For the complete essay, please visit www.sourcebooksshakespeare.com.

Acknowledgments

The series editors wish to give heartfelt thanks to the advisory editors of the series, David Bevington and Peter Holland, for their ongoing support, timely advice, and keen brilliance.

We are incredibly grateful to the community of Shakespeare scholars for their generosity in sharing their talents, collections, and even their address books. We would not have been able to put together such an august list of contributors without their help. First, sincere thanks to our text editor, Jeffrey Kahan, for his astonishingly quick work. Thanks as well to Courtney Lehmann, Tom Garvey, Doug Lanier, and Andrew Wade for their marvelous essays. Extra appreciation goes to Doug Lanier for all his guidance and the use of his personal Shakespeare collection.

We want to single out Tanya Gough, the proprietor of The Poor Yorick Shakespeare Catalog, for all her efforts on behalf of the series. She was an early supporter, providing encouragement from the very beginning and jumping in with whatever we needed. For her encyclopedic knowledge of Shakespeare on film and audio, for sharing her experience, for her continuing support, and for a myriad of other contributions too numerous to mention, we offer our deepest gratitude.

Our research was aided immensely by the wonderful staff at Shakespeare archives and libraries around the world: Sylvia Morris, Helen Hargest, and the staff at The Shakespeare Birthplace Trust; Georgianna Ziegler, Bettina Smith, and everyone at the Folger Shakespeare Library; Jane Edmonds, Ellen Charendoff, and the team from the Stratford Festival of Canada Archives; and Gene Rinkel, Bruce Swann, and Nuala Koetter from the Rare Books and Special Collections Library at the University of Illinois.

These individuals were instrumental in helping us gather audio: Ian Bradshaw, Janet Benson, Barbara Brown, Nelda Gill, and Carly Wilford.

The following talented photographers shared their work with us: Donald Cooper, Gerry Goodstein, George Joseph, Michal Daniel, and Carol Rosegg. Thank you to Jessica Talmage at the Mary Evans Picture Library and to Tracey Tomaso at Corbis. We appreciate all your help.

From the world of drama, the following shared their passion with us and helped us develop the series into a true partnership between the artistic and academic communities. We are indebted to: Liza Holtmeier, Lauren Beyea, and the team from the Shakespeare Theatre Company; Sachin Deshpandé, Victoria Baltulis, and the team from the Stratford Festival of Canada; the 2006 cast of *Much Ado About Nothing* from the Stratford Festival of Canada; Nancy Becker of The Shakespeare Society; and Santino Fontana.

With respect to the audio, we extend our heartfelt thanks to our narrating team: our director, John Tydeman, our esteemed narrator, Sir Derek Jacobi, and the staff of Motivation Studios. John has been a wonderful, generous resource to us and we look forward to future collaborations. We owe a debt of gratitude to Nicolas Soames for introducing us and for being unfailingly helpful. Thanks also to the "Speaking Shakespeare" team, Andrew Wade and Santino Fontana, for that wonderful recording.

Our personal thanks for their kindness and unstinting support go to our friends and our extended families.

Finally, thanks to everyone at Sourcebooks who contributed their talents in realizing The Sourcebooks Shakespeare–in particular: Todd Stocke, Megan Dempster, Fred Marshall, and Michael Ryder. Special mention to Melanie Thompson, assistant extraordinaire for the Sourcebooks Shakespeare.

So, thanks to all at once and to each one (Macbeth, 5.7.104)

Audio Credits

In all cases, we have attempted to provide archival audio in its original form. While we have tried to achieve the best possible quality on the archival audio, some audio quality is the result of source limitations. Archival audio research by Marie Macaisa. Narration script by Marie Macaisa. Audio analysis by Tanya Gough. Audio editing by Motivation Sound Studios, Marie Macaisa, and Todd Stocke. Narration recording and audio engineering by Motivation Sound Studios, London, UK. Mastering by Paul Estby. Recording for "Speaking Shakespeare" by Sotti Records, New York City, USA.

Narrated by Sir Derek Jacobi
Directed by John Tydeman
Produced by Marie Macaisa

The following is by permission from the Sir John Gielgud Charitable Trust. All rights reserved.
Track 19

The following is under license from IPC Media. All rights reserved.
Tracks 3, 22, 28, 37, 42

The following is under license from CBC Radio. All rights reserved.
Tracks 6, 9, 12, 21, 24, 27, 30, 33, 36, 41

The following are selections from The Complete Arkangel Shakespeare ℗ 2003, with permission of The Audio Partners Publishing Corporation. All rights reserved. Unabridged audio dramatizations of all thirty-eight plays. For more information, visit www.audiopartners.com/shakespeare.
Tracks 4, 7, 10, 13, 15, 17, 25, 31, 34, 39

"Speaking Shakespeare" (44) courtesy of Andrew Wade and Santino Fontana.

Photo Credits

Every effort has been made to correctly attribute all the materials reproduced in this book. If any errors have been made, we will be happy to correct them in future editions.

Images from the 1958 production at the Shakespeare Memorial Theatre directed by Douglas Seale are courtesy of the Rare Book and Special Collections Library, University of Illinois at Urbana-Champaign. Photos are credited on the pages in which they appear.

Photos from the Shakespeare Theatre Company's 2002-03 production directed by Mark Lamos are copyright © 2006 Carol Rosegg. Photos are credited on the pages in which they appear.

Photos from The Shakespeare Theatre of New Jersey's 2003 production directed by Bonnie J. Monte are copyright © 2006 Gerry Goodstein. Photos are credited on the pages in which they appear.

Photos from the Public Theater's 1987 production directed by Gerald Freedman are copyright © 2006 George E. Joseph. Photos are credited on the pages in which they appear.

Photos from the Royal Shakespeare Company's 1950 production directed by John Gielgud, 2002 production directed by Gregory Doran, 1996 production directed by Michael Boyd, 1976 production directed by John Barton, 1958 production directed by Douglas Seale, 1988 production directed by Di Trevis are copyright © 2006 Royal Shakespeare Company. Photos are credited on the pages in which they appear.

Photos from the Royal Shakespeare Company's 2002 production directed by Gregory Doran, 1982 production directed by Terry Hands, 1976 production directed by John Barton, and the Shakespeare's Globe Theatre production directed by Tamara Harvey are copyright © Donald Cooper. Photos are credited on the pages in which they appear.

William Shakespeare's signature (on the title page) and images from "In Production: *Much Ado About Nothing* through the Years" courtesy of Mary Evans Picture Library. Other images from the Mary Evans Picture Library used in the text are credited on the pages in which they appear.

Images from "In the Age of Shakespeare" courtesy of The Folger Shakespeare Library.

About the Contributors

TEXT EDITOR

Jeffrey Kahan (Text Editor) completed his Ph.D. at the Shakespeare Institute, University of Birmingham. He is author of *Reforging Shakespeare*, *The Cult of Kean*, and *Caped Crusaders 101*, and editor of numerous texts, including *Shakespeare Imitations, Parodies and Forgeries 1710-1820*. He is the ongoing series editor of *Shakespeare Millennium*. He has edited the poetry of Robert Southey for the University of Gloucester Press and has also been commissioned by Zittaw Press to edit the novels of the Shakespeare forger William-Henry Ireland. Dr. Kahan is Associate Professor at the University of La Verne.

SERIES EDITORS

Marie Macaisa (*Cast Speaks*, Audio Producer) spent twenty years in her first career: high-tech. She has a BS in computer science from the Massachusetts Institute of Technology and an MS in artificial intelligence from the University of Pennsylvania, She worked for many years on the research and development of innovative applications of computer technology. A student and longtime fan of Shakespeare's works, she left high-tech and became the series editor of the *Sourcebooks Shakespeare* in 2003. She contributes the *Cast Speaks* essays for all volumes, scripts and produces the accompanying audio CDs, and is currently at work the upcoming titles in the series.

Dominique Raccah is the founder, president, and publisher of Sourcebooks. Born in Paris, France, she has a bachelor's degree in psychology and a master's in quantitative psychology from the University of Illinois. In addition to the *Sourcebooks Shakespeare*, she also serves as series editor of *Poetry Speaks* and *Poetry Speaks to Children*.

ADVISORY BOARD

David Bevington (Series Advisor) is the Phyllis Fay Horton Distinguished Service Professor in the Humanities at the University of Chicago. A renowned text scholar, he has edited several Shakespeare editions including the *Bantam Shakespeare* in individual paperback volumes, *The Complete*

Works of Shakespeare (Longman, 2003), and *Troilus and Cressida* (Arden, 1998). He teaches courses in Shakespeare, Renaissance Drama, and Medieval Drama.

Peter Holland (Series Advisor) is the McMeel Family Chair in Shakespeare Studies at the University of Notre Dame. One of the central figures in performance-oriented Shakespeare criticism, he has also edited many Shakespeare plays, including *A Midsummer Night's Dream* for the Oxford Shakespeare series.

Essayists

Courtney Lehmann ("As Performed") is Associate Professor of English and Director of the Pacific Humanities Center at University of the Pacific. She is the author of *Shakespeare Remains: Theater to Film, Early Modern to Postmodern* (Cornell UP, 2002) and Co-Editor, with Lisa S. Starks, of *Spectacular Shakespeare: Critical Theory* and *Popular Cinema and The Reel Shakespeare: Alternative Cinema and Theory* (Fairleigh Dickinson UP, 2002). She has published essays on Shakespeare and film in journals such as *Textual Practice*, *Shakespeare Quarterly*, and *Renaissance Drama*, as well as in a range of collections, including *The Blackwell Companion to Shakespeare and Performance* (Eds. Barbara Hodgdon and W. B. Worthen, Blackwell 2005) and *Colorblind Casting in Shakespeare* (Ed. Ayanna Thompson, Routledge 2007).

Thomas Garvey ("In the Age of Shakespeare") has been acting, directing, or writing about Shakespeare for over two decades. A graduate of the Massachusetts Institute of Technology, he studied acting and directing with the MIT Shakespeare Ensemble, where he played Hamlet, Jacques, Iago, and other roles, and directed *All's Well That Ends Well* and *Twelfth Night*. He has since directed and designed several other Shakespearean productions, as well as works by Chekhov, Ibsen, Sophocles, Beckett, Moliere, and Shaw. Mr. Garvey has written on theater for the *Boston Globe* and other publications.

Douglas Lanier ("Much Ado About Nothing and Popular Culture") is Associate Professor of English at the University of New Hampshire. He has written many essays on Shakespeare in popular culture, including *Shakescorp Noir* in Shakespeare Quarterly 53.2 (Summer 2002) and *Shakespeare on the Record* in *The Blackwell Companion to Shakespeare in Performance* (eds. Barbara Hodgdon and William Worthen, Blackwell, 2005). His book, *Shakespeare and Modern Popular Culture* (Oxford University Press), was published in 2002. He's currently working on a book-length study of cultural stratification in early modern British theater.

Andrew Wade ("Keeping Shakespeare Practical") was Head of Voice for the Royal Shakespeare Company, 1990-2003 and Voice Assistant Director from 1987-1990. During this time he worked on 170 productions and with more than eighty directors. Along with Cicely Berry, Andrew recorded *Working Shakespeare*, the DVD series on *Voice and Shakespeare*, and was the verse consultant for the movie *Shakespeare in Love*. In 2000, he won a Bronze Award from the New York International Radio Festival for the series *Lifespan*, which he co-directed and devised. He works widely teaching, lecturing, and coaching throughout the world.

AUDIO CONTRIBUTORS

Sir Derek Jacobi (Series Narrator) is one of Britain's foremost actors of stage and screen. One of his earliest Shakespearean roles was Cassio to Sir Laurence Olivier's Othello in Stuart Burge's 1965 movie production. More recent roles include Hamlet in the acclaimed BBC Television Shakespeare production in 1980, the Chorus in Kenneth Branagh's 1989 film of *Henry V*, and Claudius in Branagh's 1996 movie *Hamlet*. He has been accorded numerous honors in his distinguished career, including a Tony award for Best Actor in *Much Ado About Nothing* and a BAFTA (British Academy of Film and Television) for his landmark portrayal of Emperor Claudius in the blockbuster television series *I, Claudius*. He was made a Knight of the British Empire in 1994 for his services to the theatre.

John Tydeman (Series Director) was the Head of Drama for BBC Radio for many years and is the director of countless productions, with fifteen Shakespeare plays to his credit. Among his numerous awards are the Prix Italia, Prix Europa, UK Broadcasting Guild Best Radio Programme (*When The*

Wind Blows, by Raymond Briggs), and the Sony Personal Award for services to radio. He has worked with most of Britain's leading actors and dramatists and has directed for the theater, television, and commercial recordings. He holds an M.A. from Cambridge University.

Tanya Gough (Audio Analyst) is the owner of the Poor Yorick Shakespeare Catalogue (www.bardcentral.com) and is on the editorial committee for the Shakespeare on Film portion of the Internet Shakespeare Edition at the University of Victoria. She taught English for four years in Japan and currently lectures in high schools and teacher training programs in Canada and the United States.